The Demilitarized Society

The Demilitarized Society

Disarmament and Conversion

Seymour Melman

Harvest House
Montreal

Deposited in the Bibliothèque Nationale of Québec, 4th quarter 1988
Second printing, January 1990

Typography and Cover: Joanna Gertler

For information, address:
Harvest House Ltd., 1200 Atwater Ave., Suite No. 1
Montreal, Canada H3Z 1X4

Canadian Cataloguing in Publication Data

Melman, Seymour
      The demilitarized society

Includes index.
Bibliography: p.
ISBN 0-88772-221-0

      1. Disarmament—Social aspects. 2. Disarmament—
Economic aspects. 3. Disarmament—Political aspects.
I. Title

JX1974.M44 1988   327.1'74   C88-090347-3

Contents

Preface:
An Open Letter to My Students,
1948-1988

Dear friends,

Even though no single one of you has asked me to do this, I have prepared this book as a letter to all of you. My reason is that I think you have a personal and professional stake in the character of our industrial economy and society. In the past you have known me to speak and write of transformation and possible decay in the basic processes that had so long yielded a fine level of productivity growth for the United States, and thereby its general industrial and economic competence. We are now in the midst of the decay that was forecast.

More than economic analysis and forecasting is at stake here. I am sensitive to the fact that you have all grown to professional maturity during decades that have included an overhang of wars, war preparing, and ever larger "defense" budgets and forces. That long experience has probably been influential in persuading many of you that these conditions are not only ordinary, but may even be tolerable—since the worst-case prospect, nuclear war, has not happened.

During March 1988 I visited the University of Idaho in Moscow, Idaho, and exchanged views publicly with Kenneth Adelman, formerly President Reagan's chief of the US Arms Control and Disarmament Agency. At one moment he told an auditorium full of high school students that they must learn to adjust to the reality of nuclear weapons; that nuclear weapons, delivery systems, and the strategies for using them, once invented, can not be "uninvented." I quickly rose and stated that slavery was once invented, and it got uninvented. The high schoolers got the point.

My problem is: by what means can the war system and the accompanying permanent war economies be uninvented?

The permanent military economy has long been viewed as a kind of "free lunch," just another sort of government spending, and therefore useful for job creation and income flows. But experience has taught that the normal functioning of military economy carries enormous "opportunity costs." There is nevertheless a real reluctance to face up to the decay that is now traceable to the war economy.

Once upon a time the federal government, as executor of the American Constitution, and guardian of business capitalism, was able to promise and deliver a rising level of living in return for acquiescence to the power, privilege and policies of the federal government. The social contract that endured for two centuries has been broken as the federal government is now the manager of a war economy that can neither contribute to a rising level of living nor deliver on its promise of defense.

As a strategy for power wielding, the war system is visibly decaying. For no one knows how to define or achieve military superiority while overkill capabilities are available to each of the great powers. The US experience in Vietnam, and the Soviet's in Afghanistan, illustrate limits of sophisticated military formations and military technology.

But why the detailed attention to politics in these pages? I would like to make a contribution to the discussion on how to move from where we are now to a much improved condition. How can we get out of this jam? Hence I try to define the nature of the "jam." Moreover, I can't get myself to accept the war system and its economy as unavoidable. That is why I am skeptical of movements of reform of the Pentagon and reform of theories that guide the use of its weapons. The generic term for the diverse movements of this sort is arms control. Plainly, these do not suit me since they are within the framework of the war system and its economy. They are, by indirection, an affirmation of a social contract that has failed.

A new social contract does not spring from the earth. Neither do I pretend to make a full formulation of a developing alternative relationship between government and citizens in the United States. Nevertheless, I am firmly minded to try and contribute to a reformulation. I invite you to join in. The ideas of reversing the arms race by mutual agreement (disarmament), and redesigning industrial and other facilities for conversion from military to civilian work, are too important to be left to politicians. That should be no surprise to you who know me from my teaching and writing. For I have tried to be a faithful bearer of the following values: the high importance of productive work for every individual and for the whole community; the high value of human life; the desirability of combining productive work with participation in decision making about production.

These are the values that led to what I have done until now, including the present book. These same considerations explain why I have lately helped form a National Commission for Economic Conversion and Disarmament, committed to researching and disseminating information and analysis about the policy systems that give promise of extricating us from the war system and the war economy. The Commission can be reached at P.O. Box 15025, Washington, DC, 20003.

Lastly, a reminder. A demilitarizing society is not utopia. A roster of inequities, inequalities, brutalities and economic and social decay long endemic to industrial capitalism remain, with this difference. The very process of demilitarizing—by well-designed economic conversion—institutionalizes democratic decision-making and decentralization, reinforces productive life-serving values, and frees up the resources needed for every sort of improvement in quality of life. Though not utopia, demilitarization makes a host of economic, social and political changes much more workable. There is a better chance for the continuation of life itself.

With warm wishes to each and every one of you, I am

Sincerely yours,
Seymour Melman

Acknowledgements

Chapter 1 (Prologue: Economic Consequences of the Arms Race: The Second Rate Economy) is based upon a paper to the American Economic Association, Chicago, Dec. 30, 1987. Chapter 2 (An Economic Alternative to the Arms Race: Conversion from Military to Civilian Economy) is based upon a lecture: Nov. 18, 1986, at the Rayburn House Office Building, Washington, DC, under the auspices of the SANE Education Fund. First in *The Seymour Melman Lectures on Economic Conversion and Disarmament.* Chapter 4 (Law for Economic Conversion: Necessity and Characteristics) is based upon papers to the *Bulletin of Peace Proposals,* Oslo, Norway, Vol. 19, No. 1, 1988, and to the United Nations' "International Conference on the Relationship Between Disarmament and Development," 1987. Chapter 6 (Epilogue: The Concealed Cuban Missile Crisis) is based upon an article in *The Boston Globe,* Oct. 20, 1987.

1
Prologue
Economic Consequences
of the Arms Race:
The Second-Rate Economy

While the arms race with its unspeakable hazards proceeds, it has generated a catastrophe in slow motion for the American people.

The United States has been transformed into a second rate industrial economy. The Pentagon degraded the growth of efficiency in US industry, first by replacing cost-minimizing with cost-maximizing as a main managerial method. Second, by pre-empting trillions of dollars of capital resources since World War II the Pentagon drained off real wealth from productive use, finally proving that even American wealth has limits.

While a depletion process in US industry was identified as early as 1965 (Melman, 1965), the full quality of that process took a while to unfold. By 1987 it was possible to identify the following characteristics of a first-rate industrial economy against which the depletion process could be gauged:

— first, the ability of the industrial system to offset cost increases of every sort by productivity growth.
— second, the ability to pay high and rising wages while producing marketable goods.
— third, vigorous research in basic science and in the technologies.
— fourth, the availability of an increasingly competent production support base (infrastructure).
— fifth, having the use of a currency of stable, meaning predictable, value.

— sixth, having the capability for organizing people for productive work.

— seventh, as a result, enjoying a rising level of living.

From 1915 to 1950, US industrial firms enjoyed sufficient productivity increases to offset a five-fold increase in hourly earnings to industrial workers, while only doubling the prices of all "metals and metal products" (Melman, 1956, p. 152). During the same period, it was characteristic that the prices of machines, notably machine tools, increased less rapidly than did the wages to industrial workers. That pattern made the purchase of new machine tools attractive on a continuing basis to machine users. Accordingly, American industry was known worldwide as well equipped with high performance, high productivity machine tools.

During a century of US industrialism, 1865–1975, US industry paid the highest wages in the world to industrial workers. The level of productivity was sufficient to offset the wage while the firms held domestic markets and were competent suppliers abroad as well. (Melman, 1983, ch. 10). At the same time there was expanding basic science research in the US, and a notable interest in the technologies such that the machinery-producing industries and their clients were well-served with a considerable flow of new ideas.

The infrastructure in the US was steadily improved. The railroad system, water supply, road networks, means of communication (telegraph, telephone, postal system), power supply, the education system—all served as a base of support for a widening and an increasingly productive industrial system. The US dollar had relatively stable, predictable value. It should be recalled that it was only relatively recently that the gold backing and convertibility of the dollar to gold were removed.

American industrial managements were also aggressively competent in organizing people for productive work with technologies that were shaped to suit managerial criteria. The idea of the assembly line, "Fordism," Frederick W. Taylor's "scientific management," national industrial unionism—all played a part in marshaling and operating the largest industrial labor force in the world.

The average level of living in the US compared favorably with that of Europe, the main origin of immigrants to America, and also showed a central tendency of steady growth despite the fluctuations of the "business cycle."

By the 1980s, these conditions have been checkmated. The core of these seven characteristics is clearly the pattern of productivity growth. It was the productivity growth that made possible the cost-offsetting, the high wage rate, the competitive price, and finally, the rising level of living. In the presence of other necessary conditions, including vigorous R&D, a competent infrastructure, a stable currency—it was the growth in productivity that was the driving factor in this set of conditions that constituted a first-rate industrial economy.

What happened to productivity growth? During the twenty years before 1970, manufacturing productivity grew at an annual average rate of 4.1 percent—nearly three times as high as the 1.4 percent rate after 1970. (Dumas, 1987, ch. 1). The ability to pay high and rising wages terminated by 1975. That was the last year in which the US industrial wage was the highest in the world. By 1980, eight European countries were paying higher wages than US industry (Melman, 1983, 1987, p. 309).

For 1977 I estimated the number of engineers and scientists *in civilian activity* per 10,000 in the labor force: US, 38; West Germany, 40; Japan, 50 (Melman, 1983, 1987, pp. 170, 171). The United States had a larger gross number of engineers and scientists. But the intensity of their use on behalf of the civilian economy was substantially less than in the case of Japan, somewhat less than in West Germany. In 1970 (last year of available data) America's military-serving manufacturing industries employed an average of 7.4 scientists and engineers in research and development per hundred production workers. In civilian-serving manufacturing, the percentage was one percent (Melman, 1983, 1987, p. 89).

The machine tool and the electronics industries have been

3

important areas where the preemption of technical talent by the military has played a part in so weakening the US competitive position, as to hasten the decline, and even disappearance of major sections of those industries (DiFilippo, 1986; Melman, 1983, 1987, Prologue). The US now lacks a modern rail system, a modern highway system in good repair (Choate and Walter, 1981). The city streets are poorly paved. Between a fifth to a third of the highway bridges in the US are rated as needing major repair. Decent housing is no longer available for millions. There is a growth of homelessness and hunger (Physician Task Force on Hunger in America, 1987). Important parts of the population draw water from aquifers that are contaminated. The national parks are in poor repair. The libraries are poorly operated. Waste disposal systems violate modern technical standards. The public school buildings of New York City require an expenditure of $8 billion for decent repair.

AFTER 200 YEARS: INCOMPETENCE IN PRODUCTION

The consequence of this alteration in the microeconomic process that has spurred productivity growth has been a major loss to the US of production capacity and competence. In 1979–80, 17 percent of the automobiles purchased in the US were imports. By 1986, that figure was about one-third. Machine tool imports represented 25 percent of US market sales in 1979–80, and 50 percent by 1987. Shoes: 45 percent were imported in 1979–80; 86 percent in 1987. The prudent understanding is that there have been comparable degrees of loss of productive employment (Melman, 1983, 1987, p. 200). This collapse of production competence has included not only smokestack, but also high-tech industries—those that depend on a strong R&D input. The high-tech group showed a favorable trade balance of $27 billion in 1980. By 1986, they were recording a trade deficit (US Congress, Joint Economic Committee, 1986).

For the first time in 200 years competitiveness in American industry is not a micro problem of single firms. Incompetence in production has engulfed entire US industries. By this yardstick Japan and Germany have won the Cold War, and the US and USSR are the losers. As a consequence of its normal operations, that preempted capital resources and installed a cost-maximizing microeconomy in US industry, the federal government and Department of Defense have spearheaded the creation of a second-rate industrial economy.

None of this is to say that the tangle of US economic problems that signal the decay of first-rate industrial status is the product of a single-cause system. Other factors surely play their part: managerial short-termism; the idea that we are a "service" economy, a "post-industrial" society in which production is, by definition, unimportant; a naive belief in an inherent American technological superiority; belief that speculative profit represents real wealth; large and growing administrative costs, unrelated to efficiency in production; a consensus that favors military spending as a way to regulate the economy; etc.

It is to say that massive, sustained military spending is, qualitatively, the single most critical factor in the cumulative depletion of the industrial economy. If it is dealt with decisively then the rest can be addressed. If that factor is unattended, then the rest is rendered unmanageable, and a process of continued decline is locked in place.

To illustrate, *The New York Times* of December 8, 1987 reported that US intercontinental delivery vehicles—missiles, aircraft, submarines—are able to deliver 11,786 strategic warheads to the entire Soviet's 220 urban industrial centers. Hence, US forces have more than fifty times overkill capability by this simple reckoning. A 75 percent reduction in the 1988 budget for operating and adding to this overkill capability would entail a budget saving of $54.6 billion (Center for Defense Information estimate) leaving an overkill capacity of twelve, not less lethal than an overkill of fifty times.

A new political-economic factor has appeared owing to the depletion of both US and Soviet economies by long-enduring military priorities. For the first time since World War II, a part of the ruling elites of both societies judge that in order to cope with domestic problems it is necessary to make substantial reductions in military budgets. Negotiation of large reductions in military budgets and armed forces are now conceivable and perhaps feasible.

Such a reversal would require a capability for eventually converting as much as $295 billion in annual US activity from military to civilian purposes. That defines the strategic economic role of planning for conversion from military to civilian economy. The same planning process gives confidence to proceed with a disarmament process.

What is the prognosis if the military economy continues to dominate in the use of capital resources, while spurring cost maximizing? The second-rate economy will then become progressively less manageable and the conditions of a third-rate economy will evolve. Professors John E. Ullmann and Lloyd J. Dumas have termed such a process the creation of a "Fifth World," undevelopment: lacking resources needed for repairing even key industries, and suffering a declining level of living (Dumas, 1987, pp. 129–130; Ullmann, 1985, ch. 2). That condition is now found in industries ranging from trolley cars to consumer electronics to shoes. As the decay spreads, then, as in an unindustrialized country, teams of workers, technicians, and managers would have to be sent abroad to acquire needed skills, or foreign staffs imported to the US to train the natives.

2

An Economic Alternative to the Arms Race: Conversion from Military to Civilian Economy

Once upon a time the United States was the standout performer, world-wide, as a vigorous, productive society, exceptionally strong in basic industries and in mass-producing consumer goods. American design and production methods set world standards in many fields.

These qualities have been the basis for a confident ideology which proclaims that the combination of technical excellence and money-making incentives is the key to growing affluence for all.

But the United States now is the scene of a drama different from that implicit in her confident ideology. A process of technical, industrial, and human deterioration has been set in motion within American society. The competence of the industrial system is being eroded at its base. Entire industries are falling into technical disrepair, and there is massive loss of productive employment because of inability to hold even domestic markets against foreign competition. Such depletion in economic life produces wide-ranging human deterioration at home. The wealthiest nation on earth has been unable to rally the resources necessary to raise one fifth of its own people from poverty. The same basic depletion operates as an unseen hand restricting America's relations with the rest of the world, limiting foreign-policy moves primarily to military-based initiatives.

The prospect of "no future" has become a permanent part of government security policies that depend mainly on the threat of using nuclear weapons. Never before were men made to feel so powerless, so incapable of having a voice over their own fate.[1]

THE "DANGER" OF DISARMAMENT

Both ordinary candor and political prudence require recognition of a widespread opinion among Americans that a reversal of the arms race contains the seed of economic distress. By 1987 there were, after all, 6,618,000 men and women on payrolls directly funded by the Department of Defense. They and their immediate dependents numbered more than 20,000,000 Americans. One step removed are the host of enterprises whose cash flow originates with the spending power of the military economy employees.

But fear of disarmament goes beyond such calculation. Since World War II Americans have become accustomed to the idea that military spending is the federal government's preferred instrument for regulating market demand in the US economy. Therefore there is fear that peace can mean a fall in incomes and an increase in unemployment. These chilling prospects are made to appear plausible in the absence of visible planning for conversion from military to civilian economy.

Domestic political considerations are also influential. The designers of the American Constitution did not contemplate the functioning of a federal government under conditions of a permanent war economy which warps the main institutions of government. Congress was not designed to be a marketing agency for firms and communities in particular states and districts, to be made hostage to the jobs, income and investments that come with military allocations.

The political fears that are linked to slowing the arms race, as well as reasons of economy, long-term and short-term, make it prudent to reexamine the characteristics and consequences of our long-enduring military economy.

THE NATURE AND SCOPE OF MILITARY ECONOMY

In 1987 1,111,000 civilians were on direct Pentagon payrolls, in addition to 2,257,000 men and women of the uniformed armed forces and 3,250,000 Americans employed in military-serving industry.[2] This industrial component has special importance for its impact on the US producing economy as a whole.

Unlike the textbook firm of industrial capitalism which strives to minimize cost in order to maximize profit, the proper Pentagon-serving firm maximizes profit by maximizing both cost and the offsetting subsidies. Such firms are the part of the industrial system where goods are sold before they are produced, where profitability is assured and where the prime and subcontracting firms are subordinate to the world's largest central managerial office.

The 120,000 employees of the Pentagon's central administrative office set general policy for 35,000 prime contractor establishments and over 100,000 subcontractor firms. The same top management controls capital allocations that have annually exceeded the net profits of all US corporations from 1951 to the present day. As control of finance capital is a prime deciding aspect of industrial capitalism, the Department of Defense central office is marked as the single most important management unit in the US economy. The same management also controls the largest single grouping of industrial employees and, notably, of engineers and scientists. Military R&D spending exceeded 70 percent of the government total by 1985.

Considered together, these are characteristics of a state-capitalist industrial economy.

Sustained operation of the military economy has effects far beyond manufacturing industry. A modern military budget is a capital fund. When used, it sets in motion the resources that are termed fixed and working capital in the ordinary industrial enterprise. Fixed capital is the money value of the land, buildings, and machinery that are used in the industrial enterprise. Working capital is the money value of all the other resources that must be brought to bear to set the enterprise in motion as a production entity.

From the comptroller of the Department of Defense we learn that National Defense Outlays by the US government from 1948 to 1987 amounted to $7,620 billion.[3] This count is rendered in dollars of 1982 purchasing power. The significance of this large magnitude can best be appreciated if compared to another category of capital values. An important measure of social wealth and infrastructure development is found in the 1982 money-valued estimate of the Fixed Reproducible, Tangible Wealth of the United States as given in the tables on national wealth in the *Statistical Abstract of the United States.*[4] By this reckoning the total money value of what is man-made on the surface of the United States (minus the clothes that we wear, military equipment, and household durables) amounts to $7,292 billion. Strikingly, the resources expended for military purposes by the federal government from 1948 to 1987 comprise a quantity of capital resources sufficient to rebuild the United States.

Consider further that various reckonings of economic obsolescence show that about two-thirds of the productive plant and physical infrastructure of the United States require major reconstruction or renewal. Two-thirds of the fixed civilian wealth of the country amounts to $4,864 billion. The capital outlay for military purposes during 1947–1987 was one and a half times the resources that would be required for this national reconstruction.

Apart from the immense magnitudes of resources it uses, the military economy has a significant functional quality. Military products do not contribute to ordinary consumption or to means of production. Modern jet fighters and nuclear-powered submarines are technological masterworks, but they cannot be used for housing or transportation or food or clothing, and there is nothing that can be produced with them.

A rounded assessment of the role of military economy requires an evaluation of its effects on the main institutional features of industrial capitalism: the core features of micro and macroeconomy.

IMPACT OF MILITARY ECONOMY ON THE MICRO AND MACRO FEATURES OF MANUFACTURING INDUSTRY

The ordinary regulations by which 35,000 prime contractor establishments and over 100,000 subcontractors must operate on behalf of the Department of Defense produce a major revision in microeconomy. The military-industry firm maximizes profit by maximizing both cost and subsidy payments. This has profound consequences for the economic institutions of industrial capitalism.

By striving to minimize production cost, the classic civilian manufacturing firm sets in motion the dynamic that yielded productivity growth, increased output per person employed. The mechanism was essentially the following: to offset cost increases the industrial firm would strive to mechanize its production operations and refine its organization; to accomplish this, it invested in more capital-intensive manufacturing equipment and in engineering talent. The resulting improvements in the productivity of labor (and capital) within the firm were the main instrument for offsetting cost increases from whatever source.

As this process operated within the machinery-producing industries themselves, cost increases (including wages) were offset in whole or in part by internal economies. Then the prices of products (including machinery) did not rise in the same degree as increases in costs (including wages). Hence, as wages rose more rapidly than machinery prices, more machinery was used in production generally, and average output per employee increased. What was seen as a sensible move for profit-maximizing by the cost-minimizing industrial firm yielded aggregate increase in the productivity of labor. This productivity growth, as suggested in the "Prologue," above, which had once made it possible for American industry to pay the world's highest wages per hour and also create products that were competitive in price and quality, was deformed as cost-maximizing replaced cost-minimizing.

During the 1970s this deformation was noticeably visible in the vital machine tool industry, whose machinery products are the basic means of production throughout manufacturing industry. Since the 1950s the Department of Defense has been a major sponsor of this industry's R&D and a major customer for its machinery products.[5] The prices of machine tools, 1971–1978, increased by 85 percent, while wages of labor rose only 72 percent. In Japan, during the same period, industrial wages that rose 177 percent were mainly offset by the cost-minimizing machine tool firms whose prices rose only 51 percent.[6] In Japan (and Germany) the machine tool industry has displayed the cost-minimizing pattern that formerly was characteristic of the US industry. This alteration of the classic cost-minimizing and productivity-yielding mechanism in US industrial microeconomy heralded a change in the competitive position of the metalworking industries of the United States, and by rapid extension, in the rest of manufacturing industry. By 1978, 69 percent of the metalworking equipment in all US industry was ten years old or older. In the auto industry it was 76 percent.[7]

As cost-minimizing in production diminished as a general characteristic of US industrial firms and as the rate of productivity growth declined, US firms were less able to serve their market. This micro deficiency soon translated into a major limitation on macro policy. It became less feasible to operate the standard Keynesian mechanism that used government fiscal policies as a ready device for regulating market demand and thereby employment and incomes. As purchasing power was rapidly promoted by government spending and other incentives, market demand was increasingly satisfied by production operations that took place outside the United States. This was a major consequence of the decline in competitiveness of US industry.

In this way a major alteration occurred in the long-enduring "business cycle" problem of industrial capitalism. The new economic problem of the United States at a macro economy level was no longer restricted market demand, but rather the incompetence of American industry to service that demand. This is illustrated by the following table showing the proportion of American consumption of various goods that was supplied from outside the United States.

Percentage of US Consumption Produced Abroad (1979–80)

Product	
Automobiles	27
Machine Tools	25*
Steel mill products	15
TV sets, black and white	87
Calculating machines, hand-held	47
Calculating machines, desk-top and printing	39
Microwave ranges and ovens	22
Communications systems and equipment	16
Integrated microcircuits	34
X-ray and other irradiation equipment	24
Motion-picture cameras (1977)	74
Sewing machines (1978)	51
Tape recorders and dictation machines, office type	100
Bicycles	22
Apparel	20
Leather gloves	37
Footwear (non-rubber)	45
Flatware	50

*As of 1982, this figure is 42 percent.

Source: S. Melman, *Profits Without Production*. N.Y.: Alfred A. Knopf, 1983, p. 200.

Since 1979–80 there has been continuous further deterioration in the ability of US industries to serve the US market. Consider the first two items in the table. By 1985–86 about a third of US auto purchases were imports. Within a few years it is expected that imports of whole vehicles, and components that are used in US-based assembly plants, will amount to half of US annual auto purchases. Machine tool imports now account for about 43 percent of new purchases in the US.

Following World War II the American practitioners of military Keynesianism were confident of their ability to use variation in military spending as a regulator of market demand and thereby of the "business cycle." They assumed that it was possible, repeatedly, to inject purchasing power into markets by military expenditure and thereby obtain short-term improvement in employment and incomes. From this short-term calculation they made an erroneous long-term inference: that these short-term maneuvers could be continued indefinitely. They did not reckon on the institutional (long-term) transformation in microeconomy that their repeated and successful short-term maneuvers would induce.

As the process that once yielded productivity growth in US industry was short-circuited by the widening practice of cost-maximizing, powerful pressures appeared to restrict what had once been a rapid and economically productive growth in industrial wages. After 1975 the high wage position of US industry was transformed. In terms of both wage levels and rates of wage increase, the United States is now a medium-wage country.[8]

Sustained operation of many industrial plants by rules of cost-maximizing had the effect of training a large cadre of administrators and engineers in managerial, design, and production practices that are viable only under conditions of accompanying subsidy-maximizing. The managers and engineers of military industry develop a trained incapacity for competence in civilian work.

Recent analyses confirm the negative relation between the

normal functioning of military economy and its impact on the productivity of civilian industry. Statistical regression analyses to account for the variability in US industrial productivity, from 1948 to 1982, show strong positive correlation between productivity and a rising relative cost of labor to machinery. However, military expenditure as a whole is negatively correlated with industrial productivity and so is R&D expenditure by the federal government, the largest part of which has been centered on the military enterprise. At the same time, R&D spending by private industrial firms shows significant positive correlation with industrial productivity. (These findings, part of research in process at Columbia University, will be reported in full detail so that they can be independently verified.)

CONDITIONS OF INDUSTRIAL DEPLETION

At the core of the depletion of US industrial competence is the declining rate of productivity growth as defined by the changes in average annual rate of increase in output per production worker in manufacturing industry.[9]

1950–1959	4.5 percent
1960–1969	3.7 percent
1970–1979	0.9 percent
1980–1984	2.3 percent

Professor Lloyd J. Dumas notes that "during the twenty years before 1970, manufacturing productivity grew at an average annual rate of 4.1 percent, nearly three times as high as the 1.4 percent rate after 1970."

An associated characteristic that has far-reaching effect on the competence of industrial production in the US is the age of manufacturing equipment. *American Machinist* reported that by 1978, with 69 percent of metalworking machinery in US factories ten years old or older, this was comparable to the age of US machine tools in 1940 after ten years of the Great Depression.[10]

In January 1985 the President's Commission on Industrial Competitiveness included in its report the following assessments:

> Competitiveness is the degree to which a nation can, under free and fair market conditions, produce goods and services that meet the test of international markets *while simultaneously maintaining or expanding the real incomes of its citizens.* [emphasis added] . . .
> It is not our goal to compete by decreasing the real incomes of our people. Other nations may compete by having low wage levels, but that is not an option America would choose. . . . Competitiveness is not a winner-take-all game . . . the goal . . . is not to create disadvantages for our trading partners, but to strengthen and better deploy the advantages America has at her command. . . . Competitiveness does not require American leadership in all economic sectors.[11]

None of these conditions, and their implication for industrial deterioration, are altered by speculations about possible spinoff from military to civilian technology. The R&D outlay of the US military economy is the largest in the Western world, and there must be some degree of application of military research to civilian use. But if there were serious, significant spinoff from military to civilian technology, the United States would not have suffered the civilian industrial depletion that has taken place. The realities of industrial depletion here are inconceivable under conditions of a significant spinoff process.

Independent studies on the relation between intensity of military research and industrial competitiveness show an inverse relationship between the variables. In principal countries of Western Europe and the United States, a high intensity of funding for military R&D has been associated with poor industrial competitiveness. In West Germany and Japan, the best industrial performers, there has been a low level of military research outlays and the greatest intensity of civil research and development.[12]

As the federal government sought to finance its enlarged military budgets by borrowing heavily after 1980, it set in motion a mechanism that effectively transferred inflation to the master commodity, the dollar. While the US Treasury borrowed on a large scale, foreigners became, increasingly, lenders to the US government. They bought US dollars with their currencies in such large amounts that from 1980 to 1985 the price of the dollar rose 75 percent in relation to the average price of fifteen principal currencies. Hence what came to be termed the "strong dollar" really meant a price-inflated dollar.

Two major effects were produced. By 1985 if US producers wished to be as competitive (in the US) as foreign producers of comparable goods—which they had been in 1980—they needed to reduce their US costs and prices by as much as 57 percent. Since that could not be done, the US suffered an epidemic of factory closings, which were hailed as a sign of a growing "service economy."

The ideologues of the American "postindustrial society" welcomed the decline of US production of "ordinary" goods, predicting that their place would be taken by hi-tech industries and their sophisticated products. That prediction, founded on little more than wrong-headed arrogance, has been proved wrong. By 1986 the US registered a negative trade balance in hi-tech products. Hi-tech industries are not exempt from the depletion process[13] that was spurred by micro cost-maximizing plus macro inflation of the price of the US dollar.

A second chapter in government borrowing to finance the budget is now unfolding: as the price of the "strong dollar" is diminished by intergovernmental arrangement in order to prevent a catastrophic drop, the purchasing power of the dollar in relation to other currencies will fall, and the dollar prices of imports will rise. But there can be no corresponding growth in US-based production because by 1985 many factories had been dismantled and their workers dispersed. With higher prices of imports the purchasing power and average level of living of Americans will fall. In that way, the deferred and concealed inflationary effect of the government's financing of the military economy will be finally expressed.

In every industrialized country, the production system requires a competent support base, an infrastructure. That of the US is in serious disrepair by any conventional yardsticks.

For example, conservative estimates of national requirements, 1983–2000, for highways and bridges, other transportation, water and sewer systems indicate a prospective need for expenditure of $1,157 billion during that period, and an estimated shortfall of $443 billion relative to prospective financing from local and federal government. These estimates do not consider a great array of infrastructure requirements other than those listed. The category "other transportation" does not include major modernization of the railroad system of the United States. Neither do the water and sewer estimates handle the closely linked task of toxic waste disposal.[14]

By 1988 it is obvious that no aspect of infrastructure facilities and services is exempt from decay: from railroads, highways and bridges, to water works, waste disposal systems and toxic waste dumps; from schools, libraries and parks, to the postal services, care of the mentally ill and housing the homeless.

The decline of productivity growth in the US, and accompanying depletion in industry and infrastructure, has been paralleled by unprecedented decline in the Average Annual Change in Real Compensation per Hour, for all American wage and salary earners:

1950–59	3.1 percent
1960–69	2.5 percent
1970–79	0.9 percent
1980–84	0.0 percent[15]

WHY CONDITIONS OF INDUSTRIAL DEPLETION ARE NOT RECOGNIZED

A series of conventional beliefs play an important part in

shielding large publics from an awareness of the conditions and the causes of American industrial depletion. Some of these ideas follow.

An economic product is properly identified by the presence of price, apart from the function of the product. With this reasoning the multiplied output of price-valued military goods and services promotes the enlargement of the measured gross national product. Economic progress can then be proclaimed independently of the fact that the military goods serve no consumption or means of production functions.

There is no separate military economy. In this understanding the military-industry firm is like any other firm: it buys and sells; has the ordinary array of officers; produces annual reports; issues stocks and bonds. This sort of emphasis detracts attention from the special cost- and subsidy-maximizing microeconomy of the military-industry firm.

Since military industry managers, engineers, and workers surely include a large quota of bright people, one can expect them to operate as efficiently or more efficiently than other firms. For the military-industry firm, however, efficiency (as in profit-maximizing) is obtained as the firm operates according to the rules laid down by the Pentagon. These are precisely the rules that lead to the design and production of overpriced, unreliable products.

Since the United States is a postindustrial society, it is altogether proper that the production of ordinary goods be left to less sophisticated countries while the United States concentrates on high technology. This expectation would lead anyone to expect that in relation to, say, Japan the United States would be an exporter of high-technology goods and an importer of less sophisticated products. In fact, reality is exactly the reverse: Japan exports high-technology products to the United States, like computer components and computer-operated machine tools, while United States exports to Japan are heavily weighted with agricultural and mineral raw materials. It is also significant that America's hi-tech industries, including those of Silicon

Valley, have found themselves in grave trouble in the competitive market place, except for the firms with Pentagon-guaranteed markets and profits.

Producing goods is necessarily less important as the United States has been moving toward a more advanced, service economy. The truth of the matter is that in order to live a community must produce. Making money may be a sufficient yardstick for the economic success of an individual because money gives a person a claim on a share of the community's goods and services. But for the community as a whole, there is no theory or body of experience from which to infer that its material needs can be served indefinitely from the outside in exchange for nicely printed currency.

The ability of such beliefs to distract attention from, and filter out evidence of, economic deterioration has been altogether impressive. Look again at the paragraphs that appear as the designated introduction to this chapter. They were first published as the opening pages of my 1965 volume *Our Depleted Society.* I devoted the largest part of that book to an ordered display of evidence on deterioration of production competence in US industry and deterioration of infrastructure and other physical and human capital. For most people the facts of the case could not be allowed to disturb cherished illusions about America as "Number 1."

Now, in 1986, by the ordinary standards of industrial competence—productivity growth, the ability to serve domestic markets, innovation in industrial technology, quality of industrial products, and the ability to deliver a high and rising level of living to its citizens—the United States has attained second-rate status as an industrial country. If the processes of depletion continue, the United States could become a third-rate nation characterized by the pervasive inability to find and organize the resources necessary to restore economic competence.

Conventional ideology and its institutional advocates have subdued attention to the scale and quality of the capital resources used up by the military economy, and the consequences for ordinary life-serving production competence. Therefore, there has been no planning for conversion from military to civilian economy within the government of the United States. In the absence of such capability it is not surprising that for the last quarter century there has been no planning for designing, negotiating, and carrying out a reversal of the arms race. That project contains the seed of political-economic panic in the absence of competent planning for economic conversion.

Every US president from John Kennedy to Ronald Reagan has opposed legislation to plan for economic conversion. All these executives have joined with the Pentagon and the military-industrial establishment that regard such planning as a threat to their power and privilege. They have been reinforced by economists and others committed to military Keynesianism as a policy instrument. Economic conversion planning would reduce dependence on military funding for short-term jobs and incomes and would surely erode support for the Pentagon budget and the arms race. Governments everywhere have resisted efforts to set up conversion programs. Until now only the government of Sweden has broken this pattern, publishing a major report on the feasibility of military-civilian conversion.[16]

For the United States the military-civilian conversion imperative is clear. The military economy is the main location of the capital resources that are required on a large scale for redeveloping economic competence in American industry and infrastructure. At the same time a popularly supported go-ahead signal for proceeding with negotiated reversal of the arms race awaits economic reassurance that can only be obtained from competent military-civilian conversion capability.

CRITERIA FOR ECONOMIC CONVERSION PLANNING

Economic conversion from military to civilian economy includes the formulation, planning, and execution of organizational, technical, occupational, and economic changes required to turn manufacturing industry, laboratories, training institutions, military bases, and other facilities from military to civilian use.

The well-defined characteristics of military economy suggest a number of crucial criteria for economic conversion planning and implementation. Conversion planning at military-industry factories, laboratories, and bases must be made mandatory by federal law. The managers of military-serving facilities are characteristically averse to abandoning the income and profit guarantees to which they have become accustomed, and they are reluctant to confront the prospect of their own occupational retraining that would be required. Accordingly, federal law is needed to make conversion planning a requirement of serving the Pentagon—whether under contract or as an administrative employee.

Conversion planning must be aimed at generating competence for civilian economic success. That means overcoming the array of production deficiencies that have been introduced as a normal condition for serving the Department of Defense.[17]

Conversion planning must be done well in advance of prospective implementation. This is owing to the well-established lead time period required for blueprinting the changeover of production operations even after a decision has been made on the choice of new products. There is no technological or economic reason why it is not possible to design and produce in the United States good quality radios, audio and video recorders and similar products—all of which now enjoy mass markets in the United States and none of which are currently in mass production in this country. Detailed study of major military electronics operations, which could convert to producing civilian electronics products, indicates that a two-year planning period is required for bringing together the necessary data on production equipment, sources of raw materials, marketing planning, recruiting of new employees, training of new staff. This means that it is operationally unfeasible to suggest that conversion planning can be left to the time "when the problem arises."

In order to assure on-site responsibility and authority for economic conversion planning the task should be put in the hands of alternative-use committees in every military-serving factory, laboratory, and base. These local committees should include equal numbers of members from management and the work force. Thus the best talent and knowledge of all the people in an enterprise could be marshaled for blueprinting a future beyond the service of the Pentagon. The management should be required to make available all data needed for redesigning the operations of the facility so that optimum use can be made of the available manpower, plant, and equipment. To ensure requisite seriousness and commitment, the functioning of this planning process should be supported out of the enterprise's own budget.

Alternative-use committees should also be free to call upon the talents of people outside the enterprise, including the staffs of regional universities and standard engineering and management consulting firms. The merit of this approach would be to put full responsibility and authority in the hands of the people on the spot. Under such conditions alternative-use committees would become the natural focal point for innovative ideas of all sorts from every employee in the enterprise. Such workplace democracy would be a powerful spur to the thoroughgoing cooperation necessary for effective enterprise conversion.

Subsidies to guarantee profitability must be excluded from converted facilities. This is essential if the cost-maximizing pattern of operation is to be transformed into the cost-minimizing pattern.

While subsidy to enterprises should be avoided, the credibility of an economic conversion process would be bolstered by the build-up of a fund from the sales of military enterprises to assure reasonable income maintenance for the people of converting organizations during a changeover period.

A national economic conversion commission must be located outside the Department of Defense. This is the only way to assure breaking the economically counterproductive cost-maximizing style of military operation. Furthermore it would forestall transforming the Department of Defense into a Department of the National Economy.

For the people working in military economy the attraction of civilian work will be much greater if they can see a network of prospective markets. There are manifold opportunities in two main directions: the first is for large-scale capital investment planning by governments at all levels for the repair of major parts of the capital plant in the US infrastructure; the second is for planning production of items that are now heavily imported. There is no technological, economic, or organizational reason why good quality shoes cannot be made in the United States for sale at acceptable prices. The idea of producing goods here to replace many imports is completely reasonable. Many Americans have forgotten that for more than a century, 1865-1975, American industrial firms paid the highest wages in the world and were able to make good quality, price-competitive products. This was accomplished by thorough-going application of cost-minimizing methods in technology and economy discussed earlier in this chapter.

The changeover from military to civilian work at the close of World War II is an important part of our social memory. It seems to have been accomplished readily enough and without special planning, except for the initiatives of such industry groups as the Committee for Economic Development that was formed during the war to encourage "postwar planning." But reconversion following World War II had a special characteristic that cannot be duplicated today: by and large, the industrial firms that did war work until 1945 went back to producing the civilian products they had produced before the war and with which they were completely familiar. This meant that production methods, product designs, sources of supply for materials and equipment, and marketing methods were all known quantities, embodied in the experience of the people who were available after the four-year interregnum to return to civilian production operations. That reconversion experience is not reproducible today. Factories, bases, and laboratories built after World War II to specialize in serving the military must be *converted*, not *reconverted*, to civilian tasks.

Decentralized methods for conversion planning and implementation deserve special emphasis because of the long managerial tradition for centralism in both private and public enterprise. Assume that Pentagon-serving facilities are required to prepare blueprint-ready economic conversion plans. Should these be subject to systematic review and approval by a national economic conversion administration? Professor Lloyd J. Dumas has examined the prospect of implementing a national administrative organization and has determined that it would be counterproductive to competent planning on several levels. It would be very costly, requiring an annual budget of over half a billion dollars. It would require recruiting a large national pool of professionals with specialized technical talent. But most important, it would remove responsibility for the success of conversion operations from the local alternative-use committees to the national body. That is contrary to the primary requirement for competent conversion planning: on-site responsibility and authority for both planning and execution.

Because of long-developed, trained incapacity for civilian work, especially among administrators and technologists, mandatory retraining must be part of the conversion process if people who have worked for the military are not to become burdens to civilian-oriented organizations. This is no reflection on the intelligence or general professional competence of the persons involved. The point is that their particular competences are synchronous with cost-maximizing and military-serving design, and not with the cost-minimizing requirements of civilian product design, marketing, and production.

To break the prevailing occupational patterns that are consistent with and derived from military economy, it will be necessary systematically to regroup people, especially in the administrative and technical occupations. Regrouping should help to break down and replace those traditional work habits and practices that were normal and acceptable in the service of the Pentagon that are destructive in the civilian area. There is a lesser imperative for regrouping production workers except where operations have been highly specialized and include major elements of indifference to cost in design and mode of operation. From long contact with military-serving engineers I have learned that an important part of their occupational retraining should be systematic study of the unique characteristics of military as against civilian economic enterprise.

Research and development operations in converting institutions will have to give major emphasis to production engineering topics that have been typically neglected under the Pentagon's indifference to cost and its willingness to accept products with low reliability. For example, the Pentagon has accepted and utilized fighter planes whose performance reliability is so poor that a third to one-half of the planes are, on the average, out of service. Such reliability would be completely unacceptable for, say, a fleet of subway cars. A breakdown rate that required maintenance of a third to half the fleet at any one time would cripple the functional performance of mass transportation and would be unacceptable both to management and the public served. Such performance in public transportation systems would be unacceptable even if the vehicles were received as a gift. Competent economic conversion will therefore require that America's schools of engineering and management pay fresh attention to production engineering topics they have long neglected in the name of identifying with the Pentagon or the service economy of postindustrial society.

A major topic in need of critical reassessment is the organization of work, specifically the "principles" laid down early in the twentieth century by Frederick Winslow Taylor and adopted throughout the world as criteria for achieving high productivity. Taylorite rules included work simplification and stable assignment of work tasks to production workers, who were permitted neither authority nor responsibility for the design of their work tasks or their integration with the work tasks of their fellows. At the same time Taylor specified that all decision-making be removed from the "shop floor" and put in the hands of managers and their technician subordinates. Because of science and engineering developments never envisioned by Taylor's generation, the present prospect is for ever greater use of computer technologies in design and production. It is already clear that with computer-assisted manufacturing productivity of labor and capital can best be optimized where authority and responsibility for programming, maintaining, and operating production equipment are assigned to people at the point of production. This entails a major break with the long managerial-hierarchical tradition of Western (as well as Soviet!) industrial management. Thus the prospect and conduct of economic conversion could become a major opportunity for introducing more modern and sophisticated ideas and practices for work organization that are associated with computer-assisted manufacturing. Economic conversion can be made into the opportunity for productivity-optimizing on a grand scale.

PLANNING FOR NEW CIVILIAN INVESTMENTS AND MARKETS

As part of my book *The Permanent War Economy* I reviewed the problem of economic reconstruction without centralism. Toward the end of the US war in Vietnam many government and private bodies prepared agendas for utilizing, in the civilian economy, the resources devoted to the war. This was called the "peace dividend." An important array of capital investment plans were devised. The most important appeared in the *Economic Report of the President for 1969* as a "Report to the President from the Cabinet Coordinating Committee on Economic Planning for the End of Vietnam Hostilities." This report outlined hypothetical capital expenditures of $39.7 billion per year to be carried on for an indefinite future in an array of public responsibility functions, with special emphasis on infra-structure, physical and human capital improvement. In March 1969 *Fortune* appeared with an article, "We Can Afford a Better America," that listed and priced a long agenda of capital outlays requiring annual expenditures of $57 billion per year. The Joint Economic Committee of the Congress prepared agendas of public facility needs that amounted to annual outlays of $40 billion by 1975. The Urban Coalition and the Brookings Institution also prepared recommended agendas for large public expenditures. More recently the International Association of Machinists and Aerospace Workers published a report "Let's Rebuild America,"[18] which defined major investments in physical and human capital including such major projects as the electrification of the mainline railways of the United States.

Among the invited papers presented at the 1986 fortieth-anniversary symposium of the Joint Economic Committee was one by Barry Bluestone and John Havens, "Reducing the Federal Deficit, Fair and Square." In this paper Bluestone and Havens showed a series of employment and income-flow gains that might be expected should certain military expenditures be reduced by as much as $35 billion and the sums expended instead on an array of physical and human capital infrastructure items.

All told, there are major and diverse precedents for planning civilian capital outlays on a very large scale in the United States. These exercises must now be regarded as "practice" for what is required to repair the damage done both to the nation's production system and to the infrastructure by the long-enduring priority to military use of capital resources. The planning of capital expenditures for major economic conversion in the United States must be highly decentralized, for such expenditures are needed not only in most firms but also in every township, city, and state.

Reliance on decentralized planning for capital outlays does not detract from the importance of formulating fully sophisticated input-output tables for the US economy, following the models developed by Wassily Leontief. There are necessarily limits to principal resources, and the scheduling and execution of capital investments on a large and continuing scale will benefit from the availability of input-output tables that help to define the limits of industrial and other capability.

ECONOMIC CONVERSION IN RELATION TO ECONOMIC DEVELOPMENT

Economists and others who have been oriented primarily to aggregate problems of economy and politics are prone to defining the economic conversion problem and its requirements as an undifferentiated part of economic development. There is no question that economic conversion is indispensable for general economic development owing to the mass of resources that have been enmeshed in the military economy. However, that does not mean that economic conversion operations can be treated without differentiation from the problem of upgrading the technical and economic competence of, say, the US steel, automobile, and machine-tool industries. The following are major differences between conversion and industrial upgrading problems.

For the military-civilian converting enterprise the specification of an appropriate civilian product is a primary problem. For the civilian industry requiring upgrading that is not much of an issue because the product is rather well defined, as in steel, automobiles, and machine tools.

Marketing operations are a principal challenge for the converting military enterprise, but a familiar field, albeit requiring sophistication, for existing civilian-serving firms. Availability of capital is a lesser problem for the well-funded military-serving enterprise but often a central problem for the civilian enterprise that must be substantially upgraded.

Management staffs in the converting military-serving enterprise are typically oversized and not conceivably affordable in civilian economy. During a visit to the B-1 bomber division of Rockwell International in 1978, I found 4,000 administrative employees at the side of 5,000 production workers. Even a downsized management staff will have to be retrained for the civilian economy environment. In the civilian enterprise due for upgrading there is also a management problem, but of a different sort. There the repeated need will be for more sophisticated management skills, as required for operating production systems that are far removed from Taylorism and cost-maximizing.

Engineers converting from military economy will require not only a major professional retraining but also, in many cases, professional relocation. During that same visit to the B-1 bomber division of Rockwell I found 5,000 engineers at the side of 5,000 blue-collar workers. I do not know of any civilian manufacturing facilities or products that require one engineer per production worker. So it is sensible to expect that major relocation of engineers will be necessary. That is a very different circumstance from the engineering talent problem confronted by civilian industries that are candidates for upgrading. There the engineering requirement is for greater numbers and for people with special sophistication in production engineering. These are the reasons why legislation for economic conversion planning must include allowances for professional relocation as well as ordinary machinery for job placement through the existing network of state employment services.

The production equipment problems of firms converting from military economy will often be very special and unmatched by civilian firms that are candidates for technical upgrading. In many important military-serving factories the production equipment is not only highly specialized but "exotic" in an economic sense—that is, designed for classes of work that are both costly and not ordinarily required in civilian undertakings.

For all these reasons economic conversion planning has to be specialized and carried out separately from, even though parallel to, civilian industry upgrading.

IDEOLOGICAL BARRIERS TO ECONOMIC CONVERSION PLANNING

There is quite a contrast between the quality of the justifications that are summarized here for legislation to mandate economic conversion planning and the fact that it has not taken place. From the time that Senator George McGovern proposed the first economic conversion bill in 1963 to the present day there has been a phalanx of opponents. They have included not only the war-planning and war-making institutions, public and private, but also many people, surely in the millions, who adhere to beliefs that lead them to oppose or ignore the idea of conversion planning. Part of this system of ideological barriers consists of those that I summarized above as obstructing a recognition of economic depletion. There is a second set of ideological barriers pertaining directly to economic conversion. These are worth reviewing, however briefly.

Military spending, though wasteful in some respects, is beneficial waste on the whole. The economic benefit is to be measured in terms of short-term job creation and income flow. This view of the matter has been popular across the political spectrum in the United States. Among the ideologues of corporate America, the benefit of cash flow and profitability to the firm owing to Pentagon spending is seen as a way of filling the periodic gaps in market purchasing power. Among the partisans of the neo-Marxist left, military expenditure is viewed as indispensable for sustaining capitalism, whose firms require profitability regardless of the wasteful quality of what is produced. I find it striking that the far right, the liberal center, and far left ignore the effects of repeated military-Keynesian market rescues. They produce the transformations in economy marked by a new long-term problem: inability to produce.

More arms mean more strength, without limit. Among Americans who are dedicated to political power through enlarged armed forces, economic conversion is seen as a way of disparaging and limiting what they see as the principal instrument of American national political power. The grim facts of nuclear overkill on all sides and the new unwinnability of major wars are disregarded.

Economic conversion planning is unnecessary, for "The Market" will cope with these problems when the need arises. The assumption here is that all the people involved will seek out and eventually find other kinds of work, and that managers of firms will seek out and eventually find products alternative to the military product. In the eyes of the employees of the military economy, the operative term is "eventually." Since the time required might be rather long and the pain of being left jobless would be very great, these people then constitute an automatic lobby against any policy moves that threaten a diminution of military budgets and activity. (In Moscow the variant of this is the claim that the Gosplan will cope with these matters. In fact, chiefs of the State Planning Commission have opposed economic conversion planning as "costly and unnecessary," as they called my attention to their successful "reconversion" after World War II.)

Economic conversion planning is unnecessary because business enterprises have a long and successful record of product and investment diversification. However, successful financial diversification into firms with similar or related product characteristics does not address the problem inherent in the specialized military work capabilities of particular enterprises, production facilities, and people. That problem is not financial but rather one of effecting a significant changeover in product, technology, and occupational characteristics.

Military industry managers, engineers, and workers are smart and therefore flexible. Even assuming such intelligence, it remains that their flexibility in work competence is restricted by the skills that they have learned while working on behalf of the

Pentagon. That is why occupational retraining is sensibly mandated, especially for engineers and managers in military industry—not to reflect on their intelligence but only to insure that they will be able to wield work competence that is relevant to civilian economy.

Economic conversion just requires giving civilian product orders to military industry, laboratories, and bases. That was precisely the assumption made by the chiefs of several military-industry firms who assigned production orders for major transportation products to various of their aerospace divisions. The consequences were uniformly disastrous as familiar aerospace technology and organization patterns were applied to civilian tasks; the results were transportation vehicles whose cost and reliability were unacceptable for civilian use.[19]

Finally, there are the core beliefs which for many Americans are part of the foundation of their nationalist allegiance. One of the most deep-rooted is that the resources of the United States being indefinitely large, the US can have guns and butter in indefinite quantities and for an indefinite future.

In the preface to my 1965 volume *Our Depleted Society*, I wrote that "it is likely that the Soviet Union has experienced a parallel process of depletion. That fact, once understood, will help to establish common ground for international agreement toward curtailing the arms race and the space marathon. For disarmament and the establishment of alternative security systems will then be understood as the indispensable act for rehabilitating depleted parts of American and Soviet society. Similar reasoning applies to other industrialized countries, especially to Great Britain." That 1965 assessment is still applicable in 1988.

The United States has a unique opportunity with respect to economic conversion planning. Attention to this topic by farsighted members of Congress since 1963, at the side of independent researches by scholars in the universities, has given the United States a coherent body of knowledge which can be used for designing an effective series of economic conversion plans. Presently, a bill proposed in the House of Representatives by Rep. Ted Weiss (Dem., New York) and his associates embodies the principal criteria considered in this chapter.

In sum, my judgment is that theories and policies on "how to live with the bomb" and how to operate military economies are a blueprint for economic decline, as well as an invitation for political authoritarianism and for lawlessness that undermine a constitutional form of government. Continuing and deepening economic and political depletion is a normal part of the social cost of such a policy system.

Economic conversion planning is part of an alternative system of policy. It confers direct economic benefit while giving confidence for proceeding with the planning, negotiation, and implementation that are required to reverse the arms race.

NOTES

1. S. Melman, *Our Depleted Society* (New York: Holt, Rinehart & Winston, 1965), 3–4.
2. US Department of Defense, Office of the Assistant Secretary of Defense (Comptroller), *National Defense Budget Estimates For FY 1987*, (May 1986), 125.
3. *Ibid.*, 116, 117.
4. US Bureau of the Census, *Statistical Abstract of the US for 1985* (1985), 461.
5. D. Noble, *Forces of Production* (New York: Alfred A. Knopf, 1983).
6. S. Melman, *Profits Without Production* (New York: Alfred A. Knopf, 1983), 174.

7. *Ibid.*, 184.
8. *Ibid.*, 309.
9. L. J. Dumas, *The Overburdened Economy* (Los Angeles: University of California Press, 1986), 11, as corrected in paperback edition. The average productivity rise, 1980–1984, had to be influenced, apart from other factors, by the extensive closing of higher-cost, lower productivity factories in many industries. See data in S. Melman, *Profits Without Production, op. cit.*, 30–35, 200.
10. *American Machinist* (Dec. 1980), 133.
11. L. J. Dumas, *op. cit.*, 235.
12. *The New York Times* (November 11, 1986).
13. W. F. Finan, P. D. Quick, K. M. Sandberg, *The* US *Trade Position in High Technology: 1980–1986*, A Report Prepared for the Joint Economic Committee of the United States Congress, October, 1986. (Quick, Finan & Associates, Inc., Suite 340, 1020 19 St., N.W., Washington, D.C. 20036.) See also the discussion on product quality and costs in US micro-chip production in S.Melman, *Profits Without Production, op. cit.*, 199.
14. US Congress, Joint Economic Committee, *Hard Choices, A Report on the Increasing Gap Betwween America's Infrastructure Needs and Our Ability to Pay for Them* (Feb. 25, 1984), 5.
15. L. J. Dumas, *op. cit.*, 11.
16. Inga Thorsson, *In Pursuit of Disarmament: Conversion from Military to Civilian Production in Sweden* (Stockholm: Liber Allmanna Forlaget) vols. 1a and 1b, 1984; vol. 2, 1985.
17. S. Melman, *op. cit.*, ch. 5.
18. International Association of Machinists and Aerospace Workers, *Let's Rebuild America* (July, 1983), (IAM, 1300 Conn. Ave., N.W., Washington, D.C., 20036).
19. S. Melman, *op. cit.*, ch. 14.

3
Politics for Peace:
A Road Map,
Not a STOP Sign

The emergence of formidable economic crises in both the US and USSR has affected the war/peace politics of both societies. For the first time since the onset of the great arms race major mutual reductions in weaponry and forces are being considered. A part of the ruling elites of both societies agree that military cuts are needed in order to cope with domestic economic problems.

In both countries the enormous cumulative drain on capital resources for military uses has depleted ordinary civilian production competence. Technically flashy arms and space race enclaves coexist with housing and food shortages, while trade and budget deficits defy the ministrations of either central planners or "unseen hands."

US and Soviet economies, independently of major differences in their economic superstructures, share processes of decay at the point of production. By 1978 the US metalworking industries sported the oldest stock of machine tools of any Western industrialized country. In the USSR *Pravda* (July 14, 1984) reported that three percent of machinery was being replaced annually—implying an average use-life of over thirty years for industrial equipment. These prosaic facts define civilian economic decay that cannot be addressed without a major conversion from military to civilian economy. For the crises of competence in production that beset both the US and USSR were strongly impelled by sustained preemption of vital production resources on behalf of economically dead-end military activity.

None of this is to say that other factors are not involved. On the Soviet side gargantuan central bureaucracies and rigid ideologies constrain productivity growth. In the US, managers oriented to profits without production, short-term planning, exports of capital and jobs, and myths about service economy damp down production efficiency.

Nonetheless, the military economies of each country have played a key role in the depletion process. In the presence of major conversion from military to civilian economy, an array of problems can be addressed. Without conversion, all manner of societal improvement is rendered unworkable.

That is why the politics of peace plays a vital part, not only for the survival of mankind, but also for shaping the quality of life.

Now, the politics. By 1985, the American peace movement had achieved major success in raising the consciousness of the American people about the special destructiveness of nuclear war. But this awareness was not accompanied by formulated programs for halting and reversing the war system juggernaut whose activities now dominate public life, and that now controls the largest single block of resources in the national economy.

By what means can the "antinuclear war" conviction be built upon to yield a politically competent, winning peace movement? That is the core subject of this chapter.

For want of a consensus on the meaning of peace and how to achieve it, the various peace-movement groups initiate a wide range of short-term actions, often narrowly focussed in scope and duration. Characteristically, the main war-making institutions are not politically targetted for diminishing their decision-power at home and abroad.

THE PEACE MOVEMENT AS A POLITICAL SUPERMARKET

During 1985–1987 I received literature from various peace organizations that called for the following short-term actions.

Stop nuclear testing. Stop the Star Wars plan. Stop the bombing in El Salvador. Stop the possible first use of nuclear weapons. Support the Great March for Peace. Stop nuclear warship-basing in New York City (and elsewhere). Stop the Groundwave Emergency Network (for communicating with submarines). Stop testing antisatellite weapons. Stop the MX missile program (at 50 missiles instead of the 100 wanted by the administration). Stop the president from breaking the limits of the Salt II Treaty. Stop military and other assistance to the Contras in Nicaragua. Stop the campaign for expanding sea-launched cruise missiles. Support the freeze. Support the summit. Stop nerve gas production. Support the Great Peace Journey (an international march to appeal to major governments). Stop the Trident submarine program (it is destabilizing). Remove US bases from the Philippines. Stop US military intervention in the Middle East.

This is a bewildering array of purposes. Imagine the position of people who decide that issues of war and peace are really important and want to do something meaningful. Which of these issues are they to select and on what grounds? And how are they to judge among the array of well-meaning, sponsoring organizations? Are they all equally important? Should they all be given membership support?

In the international arms race the weapons are important, and dangerous. So I made a list of the twenty-five most important and costly weapons systems being bought by the Pentagon. Heading the list are the Trident II nuclear submarine and missile program, costing $52 billion; the F-16 fighter plane costing $47 billion; and the F-18 fighter plane, $37 billion; the whole list is on the opposite page. This agenda of twenty-five major weapons systems adds up to $534 billion, not counting the Star Wars program. The budget for that enterprise could amount to $1000 billion, and even much more. So we are talking about more than $1,500 billion of initial purchase prices.

Imagine that an American peace movement opposed every one of these military items, say, during the next ten years and

Twenty-five Military Systems, Ranked by Total Cost.
September 30, 1987

DOD Name	Service/Description	Total System Price ($ in millions)
Trident II	N/Submarine and missiles	52,396.5
F-16	AF/Fighter plane	47,528.8
F/A-18	N/Fighter plane	37,475.4
F-15	AF/Fighter plane	37,070.2
C-17A	AF/Heavy transport plane	35,411.2
SSN-688	N/Nuclear attack sub	30,094.1
V-22(JVX)	N/Jt. services advanced vertical lift aircraft	29,662.3
B-1B	AF/Heavy bomber	27,293.4
CG-47(Aegis)	N/Cruiser	24,869.2
F-14D	N/Fighter plane	22,940.0
Peacekeeper	AF/MX missile program	22,020.2
M1	A/Heavy tank	21,860.0
DDG-51	N/Destroyer	20,117.5
KC-135R	AF/Aerial refueling tanker	12,857.2
ATF	AF/Advanced tactical fighter	12,643.4
Patriot	A/Ground to air missile system	12,605.2
Tomahawk	N/Cruise missile	11,814.6
A-6E/F	N/Attack plane	10,659.4
AMRAAM	AF/Advanced medium-range air to air missile	10,461.7
Bradley FVS	A/Fighting vehicle system	9,718.1
AV-8B	N/Attack aircraft	9,486.1
FFG-7	N/Frigate	9,477.9
Std MSL(SM-2)	N/Missile	9,381.2
AH-64(AAH)	A/Advanced helicopter improvement program	8,843.6
C-5B	AF/Second generation C-5A transport	7,427.7

Source: Dept. of Defense, OASD (Comptroller), SAR *Program Acquisition Cost Summary* (as of Sept. 30, 1987), Nov. 16, 1987.

succeeded in stopping half of them. That would be a pretty good score considering the record of the last ten years. Would that success really cut back weapons and forces sufficient for waging nuclear and conventional war? Would such success reduce the inventory of 30,000 nuclear warheads now fielded by US armed forces? Would it cut back war-making capability more than did the partial test ban or the action that stopped the American war of aggression in Vietnam? Those were real successes.

Typically, the 1985–1987 output of American peace-move-ment literature did not place any of these particular short-term actions in any longer-term context, a succession of actions to-ward a political goal defined as peace. A comprehensive politi-cal framework would be designed with an eye to holding the loyalties of large numbers of people as they see the connections between single short-term actions and the achievement of long-term goals. Thus, for elements of the 1985–1987 list of pro-posed peace actions: what is the possible succession of actions within which any one of these concrete moves is important? What is the possible ranking or grouping of these actions by some criterion of merit? Is it sensible to assume that they are all equally meritorious? For what?*

These ambiguities reflect the absence of a theory on: how to reverse the arms race; how to define the goal, the conditions of life that could be developed without an arms race.

---

*The peace movement is not alone in this mode of operation. In May, 1986, Michael Harrington, with support of many liberal-to-radical politi-cal figures, convened a New Directions Conference in Washington, D.C. The sessions (as announced) included: "Growth through Equity; Trade Policy; Life after Gramm-Rudman; The Bishops' Pastoral Letter; Direc-tions for the Democrats; The Death of the Middle Class?; Shifting Politi-cal Terrain; Social Security & Pension Reform; New Technology: Threat or Promise?; Controlling Corporate Power; Peace with Jobs; The Role of Government; Defending Civil Rights; Pay Equity; America & the Third World; Agriculture & Food Policy; Tax Justice; The Future of Educa-tion; Whither the Labor Movement?; Forces for Social Change; The Cri-sis in Health Care; Resisting the New Right; Rebuilding America; . . . and much more."

There is no mystery about linking short-term actions to long-term political goals. But that requires: first, careful identification of goals; second, an assessment of both experience and available theory to sort out actions that are effective from those that are not (and possibly ranking those that are); third, estimating the scale and quality of resources that are required for all or major parts of the necessary actions; and fourth, preparation of a working timetable for organizing and executing the program of action. All such planning must be flexible, to take advantage of fresh opportunities, unexpected events, new knowledge. Moreover, a peace movement must expect to be underfunded and must therefore strive for efficiencies that would not be required in establishment institutions whose needs are lavishly provided.

I cannot expect to demonstrate the fulfillment of this agenda in this essay, but I do expect to illustrate the main parts, notably parts one to three. Therefore I begin with part one, the goal.

WHAT IS PEACE?

After forty years of the post-World War II arms race it is not reasonable to understand peace as the absence of war and the preparation for it. For the momentary absence of war is now accompanied by comprehensive preparation for wars of all sizes on a scale that identifies war-making as the single largest industry in the American economy, indeed in the economies of all the industrialized states, and even in the main developing nations. More than six million people in the US (including more than a third of the nation's engineers and scientists) and the largest single block of the nation's capital resources are directly engaged in the military economy. War-making institutions now dominate the governments and the economies of the main nation-states—certainly of the United States.

Under these conditions of continuous and large-scale preparation for wars of all sizes, the peace movement must revise its own basic understanding of the historically traditional differentiation between war and peace.

In a permanent war economy military activity is large and continuing, and military products are counted as ordinary economic goods. We live in a warfare state in which civilian and military boundaries have been fading, and military matters have a dominant role in public life: the annual budgets of the Pentagon comprise half of the total administrative outlays of the federal government.

A peace movement in such a society can no longer limit itself to criticism of direct military combat. For this is no isolated condition but rather the continuous consequence of the dominant role of the war-making institutions in public life. Under these conditions "peace" must, centrally, mean the diminished decision-power of the war-making institutions.

That formulation, in turn, will help to overcome part of the ideological support system of the warfare state. Most people are not inclined to be aggressively warlike. For them, a series of conventional euphemisms have the effect of softening, and thereby obscuring, the meaning of the warfare state. Thus, "defense economy," "national security state," "garrison state" all help to cover up the role of the war-making institutions as major sources of short- and long-term economy decay, and as direct planners and operators of large and small wars.

The solidly justified fear of nuclear war must be built upon. A peace movement must explain that war-making which starts with conventional weapons in the hands of the superpowers or their surrogates can readily escalate to nuclear intensity as the generals of nuclear-armed states are each under instruction to win. *Thereby, it is necessary to attend not only to nuclear weapons but to the armed forces as a whole and to their controlling institutions.*

The peace movement will make a contribution to political clarity as it insistently states the new meaning of the condition we call "peace." But American peace organizations have typically proceeded from the understanding that peace is primarily the absence of military combat, especially nuclear war.

LIMITS OF FEAR AS A POLITICAL PERSUADER

The horrendous effects of nuclear war are really frightening and grip the imagination. Peace organizations have tried, in repeated political campaigns since 1945, to appeal to fear of nuclear war while proposing particular antinuclear-war, "arms control" steps that would, hopefully, arouse large publics to restrain nuclear-armed governments. As these strategies of persuasion by fear have been pursued repeatedly for four decades, an important body of experience has accumulated which the American peace movement has by and large not analyzed. At least a start in that endeavor is important as a baseline for defining what the peace movement is up against now, what could be effective politically.

The 1980s' movement to "freeze" production of nuclear explosives and delivery systems was the third such effort since 1945. The first was the anti-atom bomb movement, 1945–1950, led by the scientists who had made the bomb, and the second was the movement to stop testing nuclear explosives, 1958–1963.

In each case fear of nuclear war was wielded to mobilize public support: for "civilian" and "international" control of atomic weapons, and for world government (1945–1950); for stopping bomb-testing (1958–1963); for a "freeze" on nuclear weapons production (1980–1985). In each campaign the hopes of peace activists for triggering a halt or reversal of the arms race were frustrated—despite the success in reducing atmospheric pollution from nuclear weapons testing. An essential consideration was underestimated.

Fear is politically neutral. Fear lends itself to political manipulation.

Response to fear in a large population is highly variable. People who are self-confident, committed to defined political alternatives to the war system and its chiefs, and to a progression of actions to deflate the power of the war institutions, can be spurred by fear to act with greater vigor. But others find fear (and allied helplessness) so painful as to cause them either to "deny" the fearful prospect or to turn for comforting reassurance to authorities who promise to protect them from the fear-inducing development. Also, it is humanly ordinary to hate those we fear.

The chiefs of the American war-making institutions responded to each of the peace movement's concerted antinuclear efforts with combinations of political hate campaigns and promises to protect the populace. Thereby, the authorities defused the peace movement's efforts. McCarthyism and the allied hate-Russia campaign (especially after the Soviets made their atom bomb in 1949) defused the 1945–1950 effort. The US war in Vietnam deflected the 1958–1963 movement. President Reagan engineered the collapse of the "freeze" movement that peaked in 1984 with a two-pronged response: first, anti-Soviet exhortation (against "the evil empire") and support for US "anticommunist" wars in Central America; second, by promising to make an "umbrella" (SDI) to protect the American people from Soviet nuclear missile attack.

The managers of the war-making institutions also design fear-hate campaigns to justify their interventionist wars against Third World nationalist and reform/radical regimes. The famous "domino theory" of the Vietnam era promised fighting, finally, on the beaches of California if the plundering Asiatic hordes were not warded off in Vietnam. Ronald Reagan's fear-hate scenarios have been used to justify the extension of the US state managers' dominion over rebellious native movements in El Salvador, Nicaragua, etc.

The peace movement's repeated major reliance on fear of nuclear war as a central theme has had major unintended effects: focus on single (nuclear) weapons; inattention to the institutionalized links between "conventional" and nuclear weapons; inattention to the war-making institutions and their role; absence of formulated alternatives to the war system; inattention to the politics of peace, a succession of steps that maps a path from where we are now to a more attractive alternative future. In the absence of a political road map, "peace" is made to seem utopian, desirable but beyond reach.

While none of these movements for arms-control steps through nuclear fear produced a reversal of the arms race, the first two antinuclear movements did yield a legacy that exists to the present day. A monthly journal, *The Bulletin of the Atomic Scientists*, has published continuously. A number of national peace organizations, including SANE, the Council for a Livable World, coalition groups, a host of local peace clubs and centers, and national groupings of church and related bodies (like the Disarmament Program at New York's Riverside Church) have functioned continuously, holding with great tenacity to antimilitarist and pro-peace values. These movements challenged the credibility of the war-making chiefs and their supporting technicians and ideologues. Taken together, the various peace groups are an infrastructure around which a mass movement might be rallied, of a size and quality to change the nature of the present war-focussed national state. How that might be done is the central purpose of this chapter.

The peace movement of the 1980s can learn something from the experience of the early American reaction to the atomic bombing of Hiroshima and Nagasaki. "American Thought and Culture at the Dawn of the Atomic Age" is the accurate subtitle of an illuminating book by Paul Boyer, professor of history at the University of Wisconsin. In his exceptionally well-researched and well-written volume *By the Bomb's Early Light*, Boyer has scanned and diagnosed the spectrum of American thought on this subject from 1945 to 1950.

The reader cannot fail to find in Boyer's book the evidence of how the antinuclear weapons movement of 1945–1950 contained experience that is being repeated. Dr. Eugene Rabinowitch, first editor of *The Bulletin of the Atomic Scientists* and a key figure in the post-1945 atomic scientists' movement, concluded, by 1951, that "while trying to frighten men into rationality, scientists have frightened many into abject fear or blind hatred" (Boyer, 93).

Boyer judged that "The emotions they worked so mightily in 1945–1947 to keep alive and intensify created fertile psychological soil for the ideology of American nuclear superiority and an all-out crusade against communism. . . . their rhetoric of fear continued to echo through the culture, to be manipulated by other people pursuing other goals. The scientists offered one avenue of possible escape from atomic fear. Truman offered another. Truman won" (Boyer, 106).

The scientists' movement and its supporters relied on fear to engender support for "world government" which many of them saw as essential in view of the obsolescence of the sovereign national state caused by the bomb. But their political activities were focussed on an unlinked scattering of single, particular, short-term issues that were not related to a longer perspective of moving toward "world government." Hence: no address to the issue of power in American society; no defined political program; no "road map" that located particular actions in a sequence of actions to move toward the more desirable condition.

In concluding his history Boyer found that

> . . . Except for a post-holocaust "Nuclear Winter," every theme and image by which we express our nuclear fear today has its counterpart in the immediate post-Hiroshima period. . . . Just as one turns from the more bizarre civil-defense schemes of the late 1940s, congratulating oneself that at least we're not *that* naive anymore, NASA scientists seriously consider research on putting large quantities of human bone marrow into orbit, for retrieval after a nuclear war for the treatment of radiation victims!

> . . . The first time around, the images of mass destruction were anticipatory. . . . The holocaust scenarios of the 1980s, by contrast, are only too plausible. . . .

A further discouraging dimension to one's sense of *deja vu* is the fact that today's activists have so little awareness of the long history to which they are contributing the latest chapter. . . . We debate the wisdom of the scare tactics of a Helen Caldicott with little apparent awareness that this very issue was the subject of massive discussion—and some bitter lessons—a generation ago. . . .

Will the political energies of the antinuclear cause once again be dissipated, and cultural awareness muted, as in the late 1940s, as in 1963? Or this time, will there be genuine progress, as opposed to mere cosmetic tinkering, toward driving back the shadow of global death? Can the destroyer be destroyed? (Boyer, 364, 365, 367)

It is significant that studies of American public attitudes by researchers in clinical and social psychology have reported similar results and conclusions. Prof. Seymour Feshbach (University of California, Los Angeles,) and Prof. Michael White (Ball State University) (see Selected Readings) reported in 1986 that

There is a considerable amount of research data that indicate that persuasive efforts which rely on fear as their principle [sic] motivating force can have complex effects and can sometimes even be counterproductive. . . . If threatening appeals were truly effective, then fear of lung cancer would have all but eliminated cigarette smoking, and fear of hunger, crowding, and economic distress would have resolved the problem of overpopulation. Fear appeals have to be convincing, but if they are too convincing people frequently respond defensively by denying the threat or by not thinking about it. Research indicates that persuasive efforts that evoke anxiety are most convincing and effective when they first convince the recipient that very negative consequences are likely to occur. The message should next convince the recipient that the negative consequences are more likely if the ameliorative recommendations are not followed. But most importantly, they should be accompanied by specific recommendations for action that are perceived as efficacious and appropriate to the threat. . . . In other words, there must be something for the recipient to *do* which will lessen the perceived likelihood of the threat and, hence, reduce his or her anxiety. . . .

One of the bitter lessons of the post-1945 decades, to which the peace movement has been largely oblivious, is the repeated and successful manipulation of the fully justified fear of nuclear holocaust by the government. Again and again the chiefs of the war-making institutions have calmed public fevers by promising to control the bomb, to use it only to deter, to restrain communist expansion, to have peace through "strength" while "controlling" nuclear weapons, and by introducing a program (Strategic Defense Initiative), with the trappings and pretensions of science fiction, that claims to make nuclear weapons obsolete. Specialized nuclear weapons technologies and strategic doctrines were developed in a network of government-financed laboratories and institutes established to advise leaders on the types of nuclear weapons to be made and how to wield them militarily and politically. The most important and comprehensive of these strategic doctrines is called "arms control."

A major indicator of political shallowness in the contemporary peace movement is the naive use of the term "arms control" as a peace-movement goal.

ARMS CONTROL

Before 1960 the term "arms control" was used to refer to early, partial steps to restrain or reverse an arms race. Since 1960 "arms control" has meant regulating, managing, the arms race. That, of course, includes military escalation which can be and has been regulated and managed through international agreements. (For example: Salt II regulated a two-thirds increase in permitted nuclear weapons as against Salt I.)

The arms-control policy alternative to disarmament was invented in 1960 by a group of academics with close ties to the Kennedy White House and was quickly made into official dogma. Peace organizations have been prone to accept an arms-control identity as their tradition of single-issue short-termism made various arms-control proposals seem entirely reasonable. Here are three illustrations. First, declarations not to use nuclear weapons first are acceptable as restraint by many peace organizations despite the ambiguity of ever knowing the sequence of events in complex crises, and even though the main advocates of this policy for the US (like Robert McNamara and McGeorge Bundy) have been architects of the US side of the arms race. Second, the Salt II treaty is an arms-control issue and favored not only by parts of the US military and political establishment, but also by many peace organizations—notwithstanding the fact that the treaty authorized a two-thirds increase in nuclear weapons. Third, peace organizations have been asked to support the appropriation of sums smaller than the Pentagon's budget requests for projects like MX and Star Wars. The lesser sums would be "less destabilizing," and their achievement is hailed as an arms-control success.

Under the banner of arms control, peace organizations became involved in a basic shift of emphasis. In the name of "realism," and to escape disapproval from establishment institutions, peace groups proceeded to avoid attention to reversing the arms race, and avoided addressing the problem: what particular actions would best contribute to that result? Instead, "peace" (undefined) and opposition to "nuclear war" were to be served by one or more short-term actions, as listed at the opening of this essay.

This orientation has been encouraged, urged, and supported by an array of foundations that have given grants to the educational work of peace organizations. A similar orientation is found in the official US Arms Control and Disarmament Agency. Its Hubert Humphrey Fellowships, for example, have been awarded only for studies in arms control and military strategy; not one has been given for the study of disarmament or economic conversion. As a member of their staff explained to me: "You surely understand that disarmament is not a realistic prospect in the near future." True, but I also understand that the arms-control orientation makes a major contribution to that condition.

None of this is to imply that arms control involves a single, inflexible policy. At the outset, arms control was formulated as a scheme for assuring "stabilized deterrence" between the two nuclear-armed superpowers. That seemingly attractive result was to be achieved by arming each nation with an agreed number of ICBMs that would be very securely shielded, hence giving each nation an assured "second strike" capability. Then the rational decision-makers on each side would rule out attempts at "first strike," and stability would reign. All this was checkmated by the normal military and managerial institutional imperatives for achieving advantage, a winning combination. The idea of "stabilized deterrence" gave way to the idea and practice of trying, by agreement, to regulate, to manage the continuing arms race.

Within the framework of regulating the arms race there is room for differences: for example, would 100 MX missiles be more "destabilizing" to nuclear deterrence than fifty; should US defense be redesigned to rely on nonnuclear rather than on nuclear weapons and forces? Peace organizations that are arms-control oriented can say yes, while the Arms Control and Disarmament Agency and the Pentagon can say no. However earnestly intended and pursued, these debates take place within the framework of the arms race. Neither position in such debates contributes to diminishing the power of the war-making institutions.

The American liberal establishment that invented and propagated the ideology and institutionalization of arms control has been caught in a contradictory posture. It wants to help avoid nuclear war while continuing to support the war-making institutions and the wielding of large armed forces as instruments of government policy. The same liberal establishment has been committed to military Keynesianism—using variation in military spending as a government-controlled regulator of employment and income. Until now this has characterized the liberal wing of the Democratic Party.

Peace organizations have sought financial and moral support from the liberal establishment and its myriad institutions —foundations, institutes, publications. One of the key postures in this pursuit has been an acceptance of arms-control ideology and policy formulation. So peace organizations have frequently followed the lead of the liberal establishment on arms-control issues rather than initiating concerted efforts to challenge and diminish the power of the state and corporate war-making institutions. A serious effort to challenge their ideology and power is alien to the arms-control perspective.

When peace organizations view the world within an arms-control framework, there is little or no prospect for political initiatives against the war-making institutions. The same arms-control perspective argues for attention to narrowly defined, short-term issues, with special attention to nuclear-related weapons. The present intertwining of conventional weapons (like cannons) with nuclear warheads (in their shells) is typically overlooked. Thereby the necessity of deflating the whole war system, and not merely nuclear war weapons, is lost from view. Reversing the arms race and planning for economic conversion then become, at best, visionary ideals, unrelated to the arms-control topics whose very formulation places them and their bearers within the framework of the arms race.

By 1987 Ronald Reagan had preempted the arms control position. The treaty on removing Intermediate Nuclear Forces from the nuclear delivery systems of the US and USSR was hailed as a major success in regulating the arms race, despite the fact that it affected only about four percent of the nuclear arsenals. Indeed, the signing of the treaty was accompanied by discussion about possible sequences of steps for limiting nuclear warhead testing and for regulating (by reducing) the number of intercontinental delivery vehicles. The arms control advocates in the peace movement felt vindicated, having apparently contributed to moving the US government to take what were hailed, once again, as "first steps" toward controlling, hopefully limiting, the arms race. However, behind the glittering facade of the Reagan-Gorbachev summitry the US war-making institutions were making other plans.

A "blue-ribbon," politically bipartisan Commission on Integrated Long-Term Strategy was formed early in 1987, and recommended to President Reagan a "shift toward a strategy of deterrence that gives greater emphasis to more advanced and accurate non-nuclear weapons" (*New York Times*, January 11, 1988). Said the Commission: "To help defend our allies and to help defend our interests abroad, we cannot rely on threats expected to provoke our own annihilation if carried out." Hence, under a cover of bipartisanship that was signalled by the participation of both Henry A. Kissinger and Zbigniew Brzezinski, the Pentagon planned a strategy for new weapons and forces development even as the nuclear arsenals were being arms-controlled.

A winning strategy for the peace movement must start from an assessment of the political-economic capabilities, strengths and weaknesses, of the main opponent, the war-making institutions.

WHAT ARE THE WAR-MAKING INSTITUTIONS?

Two centuries of industrial capitalism include a history of warmaking by the US government in the service of profits and power. This serviceability has taken two main forms: the direct purpose of military operations; the methods of war-making. Defense has meant, primarily, defense of the normal capitalist (managerial) imperative for maintaining and enlarging decision-power. Therefore investing, profit-taking and seizure of direct control over entire countries (as in Central America and Vietnam) have been ordinary military-political objectives. Numerous US military interventions were explicitly directed to make, for example, Latin American countries, the Philippines, China, safe for US business investment. The titanic struggles of two world wars embraced diverse political and economic issues. But the mode of conduct of these wars by the government of the US was unimpeachably serviceable to business profits and power.

After World War II American business dominated the world economic scene. With the largest intact industrial system and vast finance capital funds, American corporations launched a foreign investment effort valued, by 1983, at $226 billion of direct foreign investment (managerial control of foreign assets, exclusive of bank deposits, loans, securities, etc., owned by Americans).

Making the world safe for these operations is a continuing concern of the National Security Council that coordinates the policies of the Department of Defense, the State Department, the Central Intelligence Agency, and the National Security Agency—with secret budgets in the tens of billions dollars, and the federal government's array of finance and banking units that service the main war-making agencies.

The Department of Defense alone has over a million civilians on its own payroll. A joint Chiefs of Staff operation and an Office of the Secretary of Defense—with several thousand staffers—dominate the Pentagon institutions. They govern the lives of two million people in the uniformed armed forces; they operate more than five hundred large bases in the US and abroad and a chain of college and university-level institutions that now include even a medical school as well as the traditional service academies and war colleges. By the early 1980s the DOD received an annual allocation of capital that was half as large as the money value of all new civilian capital formation in the American economy.

Outside the formal boundary of the federal government there is the great network of prime and subcontracting factories and firms that serve the Pentagon. Then there are the Pentagon-serving laboratories in industry and in "nonprofit" research institutions, including parts of the universities.

For more than a quarter century the universities have been producing specialists in mind-bending militarized theories and ideologies. The "defense intellectuals" owe their place in society to their accomplishments as theorists of military threat systems and as planners of smaller and larger human carnage. Nothing is more threatening to the professional status of these "experts" than the success of a peace movement.

But the capabilities of these institutions for bolstering profit, income, employment, and ideology are not a sufficient description of the war-making institutions. For the Pentagon of World War II and after was significantly altered during the 1960s under the presidency of John F. Kennedy. A new state management was installed in the federal government. This is the summary description and analysis I gave in the opening pages of my *Pentagon Capitalism*.

> In the name of defense, and without announcement or debate, a basic alteration has been effected in the governing institutions of the United States. An industrial management has been installed in the federal government, under the Secretary of Defense, to control the nation's largest network of industrial enterprises. With the characteristic managerial propensity for extending its power, limited only by its allocated share of the national product, the new state-management combines peak economic, political, and military decision-making. Hitherto, this combination of powers in the same hands has been a feature of statist societies—communist, fascist, and others—where individual rights cannot constrain central rule. . . .
>
> The creation of the state-management marked the transformation of President Dwight Eisenhower's "military-industrial complex," a loose collaboration, mainly through market

relations, of senior military officers, industrial managers, and legislators. Robert McNamara, under the direction of President John Kennedy, organized a formal central-management office to administer the military-industrial empire. The market was replaced by a management. In place of the complex, there is now a defined administrative control center that regulates tens of thousands of subordinate managers. . . . By the measure of the scope and scale of its decision-power, the new state-management is by far the largest and most important single management in the United States. There are about 15,000 men who arrange work assignments to subordinate managers (contract negotiation), and 40,000 who oversee compliance of submanagers of subdivisions with the top management's rules. This is the largest industrial central administrative office in the United States—perhaps in the world. . . .

. . . Thereby, the federal government does not "serve" business or "regulate" business. For the new management is the largest of them all. Government *is* business. That is state capitalism.

My 1970 estimate of the size of the Pentagon's central administrative office is out of date. By 1985 the Pentagon's own apparatus for "acquisition" of its materiel included 120,000 men and women. I know of no comparable central management operation of this size in any other country. But numbers of people are a partial measure of the decision power that is wielded by the main directorate of the US war-making institutions.

The importance of a business firm's management is gauged by the capital that it controls. This is often measured as the money (finance capital) at its disposal, or the money value of the total assets that are controlled.

In terms of finance capital the state management is without compare. Since 1951, the *yearly* fresh finance capital funds budgeted to the Pentagon have exceeded the combined net profits of all US corporations. The assets of the 35,000 prime contractors and of over 100,000 subcontracting firms that are deployed under the Pentagon's control exceed by far the assets controlled by any other single management or possible conglomeration of firms.

The state management—because it is a management—operates with the normal managerial imperative to enlarge its decision power by extending the scope and intensity of its control. For this purpose it is uniquely situated. It holds the main levers for wielding the military and allied industrial and political power of the US. When Ronald Reagan, Caspar Weinberger, and George Shultz appeared on TV on April 14, 1986, to announce the military strikes against Libya, that was a display of the top decision-power of the American state managers; those three are the 1986 chief executives of the US war-making institutions.

The president of the US is, operationally, chairman of the board of the state management—as well as commander-in-chief of the armed forces and chief of the executive branch of the federal government. The behavior of President Reagan (and his predecessors) embodies both the traditional support for the security of foreign economic operations by American firms and the managerial power-extension interests of the state management of which Reagan is the Chief Executive Officer. To illustrate: the US government's operation in Central America and the Philippines reflects both classes of interest.

Thus, the scale of the Carter-Reagan military budget escalation is explicable in terms of these imperatives, though not on military-technical grounds: as more weapons for more military power. The enlargement of nuclear forces (in the overkill range) and the Strategic Defense Initiative (Star Wars) are irrational in terms of yielding significant military advantage. But the expenditure of hundreds of billions of dollars for these activities makes solid sense as the cash flow that is generated for the state management and its industrial empire facilitates the expansion of decision-power that necessarily accompanies these enlarged and centrally controlled operations. Thereby, the power of the state management, at the pinnacle of the US war-making institutions, is massively reinforced, utilizing the unique combination of political and economic authority to fulfill the normal managerial imperative for enlarging decision-power. The Star Wars program alone would make the state managers the controllers of the largest group of scientists and engineers ever directed by one top management.

If the SDI program proceeds as planned, it will have profound consequences for depleting the reservoir of scientific-engineering talent available to civilian economy. That is why—early on—the state managers have launched a massive, national campaign of outright disinformation and exaggeration on the "spinoff" for civilian uses that may be expected from Star Wars: all that to justify the expansion of *their* economy, regardless of the accumulating judgment on the inherent unworkability of the Strategic Defense Initiative.

The powers of the war-making institutions extend well beyond these realms. As shown by Marcus Raskin in his diagnosis of "Democracy Versus the National Security State," (see Selected Readings) the built-in capacities for authoritarianism, secrecy, and violence in these institutions have spilled over into violations of American law and constitutional principle on a large scale. The warfare state is no longer an ideological abstraction, but an increasingly precise portrait of American society. In this framework the state management has a leading role as controller of the domestic war-making institutions and economy and as final power-wielder in the US imperial system. Thereby the state management is the main planner for US wars of intervention.

The chiefs of the war-making institutions combine top political, military and economic decision-power. The US constitution confers top military power in the president, as commander-in-chief of the armed forces, and top political power as chief of the executive branch of the federal government. But top economic power is nowhere conferred by the constitution. Top control by the president in the economic sphere was a derived effect from the operation of a permanent military economy that made the president the chief executive officer of the state management controlling the largest single block of capital resources, including the largest aggregation of industrial facilities in the economy. Thereby a core feature of a leninist state design was installed in the federal government—top economic, political and military power in the same hands, often unconstrained by law. Such a concentration of powers is a far cry from the stated purposes of the Founding Fathers, as in *The Federalist Papers*, that gave repeated emphasis to limitation and separation of powers, checks and balances, and the rule of law.

Targeting those state managers and the war-making institutions politically, for reduction of their decision-power is the most significant single objective toward achieving a reversal of the arms race and sorely needed economic repair in the US. Unlike the managers of purely civilian-serving firms, or the managers of the "private" firms of the war-making institutions, the state managers and their governmental organizations require approval through political processes for their money and powers. Moreover, the state management is the single most important concentration of decision-power in the governance of the specific war-making institutions and in the top decision-making group [ruling class] of American capitalism.

The strategic requirements for deflating the power of the war-making institutions are disarmament and economic conversion.

Disarmament is the political process for diminishing the decision power of the war-making institutions, following international agreements on arms reduction. It means reducing their budgets and weapons; it means reducing the number of people —civilian and uniformed—under their control. Crucially, disarmament means reducing their control over means of production of every kind—factories, laboratories, schools. The authority of the war-makers in these economic spheres, when combined with formal political position, gives them the ability to organize for and to make war—their preferred instrument for enlarging their decision-power over populations and competing war-makers. Thanks to a near-total blackout on public discussion of disarmament since 1962, the American people are ill-equipped to understand the possible characteristics and problems of reversing the arms race. Thus: the process is cumulative. Success in the first step encourages the next one. As successive, programmed moves are completed, they change the "stage" on which the next moves are to be made. The process is likely to be long; the Marcus Raskin 1986 plan is a fifteen-year program during which important armed forces and weaponry will exist. Nevertheless, many people respond to references to "disarmament" with fear of being helpless, naked. We have become so accustomed to the world as dangerous, full of violence that it frightens many Americans to think of a US government and a world without heavy weapons. Fortunately, it is conceivable to embark on a disarmament process, being alert to ongoing issues, even as full solutions to all possible problems are not available. Are there risks in such a perspective? Of course. But these can be weighed against the known and horrendous risks of an escalating arms race.

The full disarmament agenda of an American peace movement will have to include some neglected topics: ways of initiating a disarmament process even before a full international program has been agreed upon; the role of the US when armed force is not available as a "master card" to buttress the US government and its leading corporate partners as dominant movers in world finance, and to buttress the dollar as the main currency of international transactions; the international economic position of the US in the absence of military supremacy and dollar diplomacy; the internal shape of a US government in a disarmed world—i.e., without the present DOD, CIA, NSA, etc., etc.; the external quality of a US government in a disarming world—for example, the mode of US relations with the countries of Western Europe whose sovereignty has been abridged as a virtual automatic consequence of American dominance over military security policy.

Reducing the power of the US war-making institutions should be seen as central to the peace and allied life-serving purposes of the American peace movement. Discussion about making peace that does not deal with the reduction of the decision-power of the war-making institutions is not to the point.

Economic conversion is the process of reducing the economic decision-power of the war-making institutions. This is to be done by mandating a planning process for the changeover from military to civilian work in factories, laboratories, and military bases. The economic conversion bill sponsored by Rep. Ted Weiss (Dem., NY) (and fifty-four colleagues at this writing) would set up a highly decentralized planning process based upon alternative-use committees to do the necessary blueprinting. Half of each alternative-use committee would be named by management, the other half by the working people. The bill provides for support of incomes during a changeover, allowances for occupational retraining and family relocation, health and allied insurance. At the national level a commission chaired by the Secretary of Commerce would publish a manual on local alternative-use planning and would encourage federal, state, and local governments to make capital investment plans. The latter would comprise, effectively, new markets for many classes of goods, especially the capital goods required for infrastructure repair.

Four principal functions are served by economic conversion. The planning stage itself—prior to implementation—offers assurance to the working people of the war economy that they can have an economic future in a society where war-making is a diminished, even a disappeared, institution. That expectation is bound to encourage support for the military-political negotiations for phased reduction of armed forces (disarmament).

The second function served by economic conversion is reversing the process of economic decay in US manufacturing in particular, as well as in the rest of US economy.

The Weiss bill for economic conversion contains a crucial provision for general economic development. The National

Commission established by the bill is empowered to facilitate planning for capital investments in all aspects of infrastructure by governments of cities, counties, states, as well as by the federal government. Repair of the infrastructure physical plant (roads, railroads, water works, schools, parks . . . etc.) will require outlays in excess of $3,000 billion. The direct and indirect effects of such expenditures will reach into every industry, enlarging market demand (and employment) for capital goods and consumer goods of every sort. Repair of the US infrastructure plant and equipment alone will require fixed working capital exceeding ten years of Pentagon budgets.

Third. The bill includes provision for capital investment planning by cities, counties, states and the federal government for repairing and upgrading all aspects of the abovementioned infrastructure. The national scale of such a capital investment program, exceeding $3,000 billion, will therefore comprise a massive program of new jobs and new markets.

Fourth. The national network of alternative use committees will constitute a substantial gain in decision-power by all the working people involved. Private and state managers will be paralleled by well-informed representatives of working people who have shared data and responsibility under the terms of the bill for preparing workable plans for viable functioning in civilian markets.

Against the background of these formulations of the core of a peace process, the political problem is essentially: what is the feasible pattern of action for moving from where we are now into a peace process?

To Reduce the Power of the War-Makers

Concretely, what will be required to reduce the power of the US war-making institutions: the scale of the effort? the character of the effort?

First, scale. The size of the political movement needed to

cause Congress to pass an economic conversion bill and take
allied disarmament and economic development action must in-
volve as much as two-thirds of the American population. Such
a majority, organized in support of well-defined concrete measures, is the right order of magnitude for political effect.

By what means could such a majority be mobilized? There is
already a substantial population aware of, and fearful of, nuclear and other wars and their consequences. But that alone has
not sufficed to galvanize them into sustained, relevant action.
Something must be added to evoke firm, sustained commitment and set people in motion along a logically defined path of
actions targeted at the war-making institutions.

Forty years of a permanent war economy in the United
States has caused marked erosion in production competence
and the quality of life. Mainstream economists of all stripes
have typically ignored or failed to see that connection. Conventional wisdom has held that the US could have guns and butter
(didn't a president, Lyndon Johnson, say so?); its resources
have been viewed as unlimited; and the military economy's
money-spending has been seen, not as a long-term drain on resources, but as a short-term boon for profits, jobs, and incomes.

However, by 1987 it is plainly visible that there is no money:

to modernize US civilian industry
to build a modern rail system
to retrain unemployed for new occupations
to conduct the range of research needed to raise the productivity
   of US industry
to lower the infant mortality rate
to operate medical research facilities at a high level
to care for the mentally ill
to maintain a modern highway system
to keep city streets well paved
to repair unsafe bridges
to erase poverty as an epidemic condition in the US
to feed the growing population of hungry Americans
to care for older Americans living in poverty

to supply minimally decent housing for all Americans
to stop the pollution of the air we breathe
to make our drinking water clean
to modernize air traffic control
to clean the rivers and lakes
to decontaminate industrial waste dumps that pollute soil and
    water
to conserve the national parks
to cope with waste disposal
to rebuild the city water mains
to operate good quality city parks
to provide afterschool care for children of working mothers
to raise the salaries of teachers to attract high-caliber people to
    train the young
to equip our schools (all levels) with modern equipment to better
    introduce students to the world of work
to operate public libraries at a quality level
to continue the Library of Congress as a first-class institution
to teach the functionally illiterate
to encourage able young people to go through the universities so
    that their talents could benefit the wider community
to provide day care for preschool children
to provide a nutritionally adequate school breakfast and lunch
    program

There is more and more and more.

Every one of these areas of deficiency degrades the quality of our lives. The impact is not only on the vast populations affected, but also on important groups of people of all occupations whose working lives are demeaned by severe restrictions on the resources needed to do their jobs.

Until now these areas of decay in our lives have been seen as separated, unconnected. In fact they are joined, closely linked by the common source of their resource depletion, the largest capital fund in the US economy, the military budget. The sum of US military budgets from 1947 to 1987 (in 1982 value dollars) is $7,620 billion. This enormous magnitude can be compared with the 1982 value of the Fixed Reproducible National Wealth of the US (excluding military materiel and consumer, household durables) amounting to $7,262 billion. In a word, the military enterprise has used up resources (customarily designated "fixed" or "working" capital) more than sufficient to renew the largest part of the man-made fixed assets on the surface of the US. If we assume that only two-thirds of the industrial and infrastructure facilities of the US require replacement for modernization, then the resources preempted for the military are one and a half times that quantity of capital.

It is now a strategic task of an American peace movement to make these connections between economic decay and the cost of militarism, and between economic conversion and the prospect for a full employment economy. This is an essential move toward marshaling the tens of millions of people who together can turn this country around politically and economically.

As all these people are shown the connection between the depletion of their occupations and the resources appropriated for the war economy, a new political reality will be discovered. *A coalition of all these people and the organized groups that represent them is the right size to challenge and win a victory for the majority of American people against the war-making institutions.*

Every one of the great array of organizations that will be a natural part of the pro-peace coalition has its own special goals. But for every group there will be these solid reasons for joining: cutting down the power of the war-making institutions affords the best chance for gaining the resources needed for its particular objectives; further, each group in the pro-peace coalition will swiftly discover that the coalition participants are well-disposed to take seriously and be supportive of each group's particular goals.

Second, the character of the effort that is required to achieve this goal. No new organization is needed. A coalition must be formed whose participant groups join in agreed common action demanding: disarmament; economic conversion planning; and reallocation of resources for economic development. At the side of these common action demands, each participant group can define the connection between its special purpose and program, and the peace coalition actions. The "social glue" that will bind together the diverse groups of this coalition will be the understanding that when the economic conversion and disarmament issues are dealt with, then the particular problems of each coalition member can be addressed. The converse is obvious: there is little chance for either life or social justice in a warfare state. There will have to be ways for efficient, speedy communications and tactical decision-making. But all that should be workable against a background of agreement on basics. For example, once there is agreement on making support for the coalition's goals a prime criterion for backing candidates for public office, each participant group will find, develop, and apply its own ways of carrying this out.

PREPARING FOR ECONOMIC DEVELOPMENT

The partners in the peace coalition who represent depleted industries, infrastructure and human services activities that are in disrepair will have a natural interest in formulating workable plans for economic development, more exactly, "real" economic development. This qualification is needed as economic development is most often taken to mean more money-valued activity, regardless of the nature of the product. For the present discussion I mean civilian economic growth, civilian goods, civilian services. Military activity, while money-valued, has no civilian use-value and hence does not qualify as the economic development that is required. The most straightforward approach will be possible for activities that are well understood as public responsibility. Budgets for large capital outlays and good maintenance will have to be developed at town, city, state, and federal levels for all aspects of infrastructure. Policies will have to be formulated for the reallocation of funds from reduced military budgets.

A more complex set of problems will be connected with re-constituting near bankrupt enterprises in depleted industries, and with establishing new enterprises in industries that have almost or entirely disappeared from the US scene. Depleted in-dustries are characterized by the withdrawal of management from production responsibility. In these realms there will be a need for addressing options that go far beyond conventional ideas about subsidies of various sorts as incentives to management.

In many US industries management has abandoned produc-tion completely or transferred production abroad. How can the working people with a stake in American production organize themselves as competent working and decision-making groups? What are workable models for this purpose? In fact worker-owned enterprises in the US and abroad include an array of highly competent enterprises in sophisticated industrial set-tings. (See the Selected Readings list.) What options are avail-able for the vital finance capital without which major new investments are impossible, even in the presence of competent organization of work? If the commercial banks and investment bankers are ill-disposed toward worker-owned enterprise, then what is needed to tap the finance capital now contained in the pension funds of trade unions and other organizations of work-ing people? By 1985 there were more than $500 billion in these funds.

These problems of economic development will become much more addresssable in a society that has an economic conversion planning mechanism in place. For the operation of alternative-use committees will, automatically, train a large number of managers, engineers, and workers in the problems of designing industrial and other enterprise. And the economic conversion mechanisms for retraining engineers and managers will make them available in large numbers for fresh responsibilities in ci-vilian spheres.

THE PEACE MOVEMENT AND THE STATE

In the long tradition of Western political movements that have been deeply critical of state policies, the opposing movements have usually become competitors for state power. They have sought to replace the state administrators with their own people. A different perspective is implied by the reasoning of this discussion.

The American peace movement must aim to change the character of the state. That is the meaning of diminishing the power of the war-making institutions. Changes in personality, party, or ideology of government office-holders are necessarily subordinate to the task of diminishing the war-making institutions and replacing them with life-supporting institutions. Stated differently: *the peace movement is not a competitor of the present managers of the war-making institutions, seeking to replace them with a new staff.* The peace movement aims to diminish, and finally to remove, these institutions and thereby change the very character of the state.

This is a very different perspective from that of state socialist or state capitalist political movements. For the ideology of such movements has typically viewed the capture of control over the state, especially the central government, as indispensable for the achievement of their main objectives. By contrast, the objective of reducing the decision-power of the war-making institutions means reducing the power of the central government.

Many Americans have failed to qualify a lesson learned during the Great Depression. At that time the federal government appeared to be the last available source of competent authority when businesses and local governments suffered political-economic collapse. In response to that crisis a heavy majority consensus supported unprecedented centralized power-wielding by various agencies of the federal government. But a population of 240 million cannot be detailedly managed from a central office. Sheer limits on administrative feasibility, plus an interest in

democratic participation suggests the importance of developing
ways of setting national standards for many activities, with decentralized implementation. Centralized managerial operations, it should be noted, are counterproductive for competent
repair of the great array of infrastructure activities that are in
disrepair.*

Every aspect of economic conversion planning and implementation will require unrelenting care to safeguard the process against pressures for centralism and subsidy. For these
practices are core components of the shockingly normal technical unreliability and ballooning costs and prices that character-
ize military industry and its products (see Chapter 11 of my
Profits Without Production). The managers, engineers, and
production workers of the military economy have had long experience as wards of the government. Trade associations, engineering societies, and trade unions have become trained into
ways of working that include strong dependence on federal
government subsidy and initiatives of every kind. So it is no
surprise that representatives of such bodies should try to define

---

*See also the formulation of this position by Mary Kaldor, *Bulletin of
Peace Proposals*, Vol. 16, No. 4, 1985, "Transforming the State: An Alternative Security Concept for Europe." She wrote:

> Unlike previous anti-systemic movements, the peace movement
> does not view the State as an instrument for carrying out its ob-
> jectives. Or to put it another way, the peace movement does not aim
> to capture State power. Rather, the peace movement aims to change
> the nature of State power, to change the form of social relationships
> that constitute the State, so that the State is responsive to popular
> demands. Whereas previously successful anti-systemic movements
> found themselves constrained by the nature of the State and inter-
> State relations so that they were unable to carry out fully pro-
> grammes of social transformation, the peace movement aims to
> constrain State power. The way in which the US anti-war movement
> succeeded in forcing a right-wing government to end the war in
> Vietnam is an excellent example of such a strategy. . . .

economic conversion as a shift from one federal agency to another for the receipt of subsidy and for dependence on top managerial government control. But reliance on subsidy to converting enterprises removes pressures for occupational retraining and organizational regrouping, and encourages continuation of the ways of working that welcome cost-maximizing and discourage attention to the production of good quality products at acceptable prices. The disastrous consequences of such practices have been repeated wherever subsidy has accompanied attempts by factories with long Pentagon service to make civilian products (see the accounts in Chapter 13 of my *Profits Without Production*).

A national coalition for peace that is equipped with plans for disarmament, economic conversion, and economic development will have the political clout for finally denying to the warmaking institutions the money and other resources that they have become accustomed to. Closing the finance-capital flow is decisive, but not sufficient. A further requirement is the planning and execution of occupational and enterprise conversion, including major relocation of technologists and administrators from military economy, where they are present in oversize proportions unnecessary in civilian enterprise.

Disarmament and economic conversion prepare the way for large-scale reallocation of the capital resources long assigned to economically nonproductive military functions. The same developments facilitate decentralized ways of controlling political-economic affairs and reducing the powers of the giant state-managerial and corporate centralized hierarchies. Regional, state, and city organizations can be endowed with all the technical competence required for organizing complex operations, as in infrastructure planning and operation. Within limits of agreed national standards, like quality of water supply, the decentralized mode of operation yields a major advantage—superior knowledge of actual local conditions for which new enterprises and rebuilt services must be compatible. By contrast, one of the built-in deficiencies of centralized economic/

industrial authority is poor knowledge of specific local conditions and a consequent vulnerability to inappropriate technical, economic, and organizational decisions.

Until now the fear of an alien enemy has been added to the economic weaknesses exemplified by the Great Depression, in order to justify a warfare state, with its high degree of centralized authority, lessened local control and personal liberty at the side of a huge military economy. But the contradictions between a permanent war economy and economic well-being have finally become unbearable to important parts of both American and Soviet ruling elites. Hence the beginnings of arms reductions in the Intermediate Nuclear Force treaty of 1987 and the Reagan-Gorbachev "summit" meeting in Washington that showed off Soviet leaders with a "human face."

Having outlined a statement of peace-movement goals and an economic and disarmament strategy, now political methods: first, the strength and limitations of unlinked short-term actions; second, how to link short-term action to long-term goals.

POLITICAL GAINS FROM CONCRETE SHORT-TERM ACTIONS

What political gain can be expected, at best, from a succession of short-term, but unlinked, objectives? Clearly defined, concrete goals can be readily understood by people who are pragmatic and not necessarily versed in political theories or the history of militarism. Thus: stop nuclear testing; stop US intervention in Nicaragua; stop the B-1 bomber; stop the Trident program, etc. People new to such issues can quickly pick up essential facts, understand the immediate implications of many of these proposals, and then be participants in the array of political actions that are undertaken for each goal.

Also, personal participation in the practical work for these or related short-term goals can potentially broaden the perspective of the activated person. Each issue can be seen to have not only military and political but also economic, technical, and other aspects. Thereby intellectual horizons are enlarged.

The campaigns on such issues bring each participant into collision with visible political operations of the war-making institutions as they use, for example, their influence over the mass media to press their case and strive to put down the pro-peace efforts. An alert participant on the pro-peace side can see the power-wielding on the other side. This can spur many people to better appreciate the quality and depth of the power wielded by the war-making institutions.

But these gains are rarely consolidated in long-term participation in the peace movement. The various peace organizations do not usually accompany action on single issues with background analyses of the origins of issues, and explanations of linkage to further actions on a road map that leads toward peace, diminished power of the war-makers. Peace organizations suffer high attrition and turnover rates as members are not encouraged to see themselves as long-distance "political runners" who undertake short-term actions in a continuing, directed political stream that is pointed to the long-term goals of reversing the arms race and the decision-power of the war-makers.

POLITICAL LIMITATIONS OF SINGLE-ISSUE SHORT-TERMISM

SANE, the National Committee for a Sane Nuclear Policy, was founded to organize support for a treaty to ban testing of nuclear explosives. From 1958 to 1963 (when the partial test-ban treaty was negotiated) the people of SANE typically believed that the test-ban treaty would be a first step to peace. In some undefined way achieving this treaty would propel a succession of further events comprising a reversal of the arms race.

In fact, there was no next step. There was neither an automatic nor a planned succession of actions. Nothing is a "first step" unless subsequent acts are automatically set in motion or are deliberately programmed. Neither occurred.

The Vietnam war was stopped. Many peace activists believed that peace had arrived, that success in stopping the US war in Vietnam was surely a "first step." Actually, as the anti-Vietnam organizations largely faded away, the managers of the war-making institutions regrouped, so that by the 1980s they were fully retooled and reorganized for fresh rounds of wars of intervention.

Even the story of the US war in Vietnam has been blotted out. Students in my classes during the 1980s have had little idea what happened in Vietnam. They were not taught in the high schools; they were not taught in the colleges; they haven't heard about *The Pentagon Papers*, the official history of the US government's war in Vietnam. I recently asked a group of twenty graduating seniors: "How many of you know who Robert McNamara is?" Two hands went up. The others had never heard of him.

An American peace movement has been functioning these last decades, and the college generation doesn't know the part played by the peace movement in stopping the US government's war, who headed the Pentagon and was in charge of escalating and operating the war in Vietnam. They don't know that this man fashioned state capitalism on a scale previously unheard of in the government of the United States, that he saw to the installation of a thousand Minute-Man missiles, even as he denied the existence of nuclear overkill.

Evidently even a series of successes in unlinked pro-peace operations can leave the war-making institutions with their decision-power intact; their budgets, their organization, and especially the ideological support system unimpaired. Recall that the test-ban treaty was accompanied by agreements with the Joint Chiefs of Staff to make available more funds, more manpower for nuclear weapons development. So *after* the partial (atmospheric) test-ban treaty was signed, there was more nuclear weapons testing than ever before.

Noam Chomsky speaking in Boston (April 1985) on "The Manufacture of Consent," commented on short-termism and narrowly formulated political goals in the peace movement, saying

> ... such resistance, while sometimes effective in raising the costs of state violence, is of limited efficacy as long as it is not based on understanding of the forces at work and the reasons for their systematic behavior, and it tends to dissipate as quickly as it arises. At the same time, a frightened and insecure populace, trained to believe that Russian demons and Third World hordes are poised to take everything they have, is susceptible to jingoistic fanaticism. . . .

So with the stopping of the US war in Vietnam no large population was trained to understand how that war came about, the role of the state managerial institutions, and what could be expected of them in the future. Lacking those understandings, the anti-Vietnam war movement dissipated. That war was dealt with mainly as a short-term, narrowly defined issue, as though a unique event in American history.

Short-term perspectives and narrowly defined issues have been further reflected in the main literature offerings that come from peace organizations and from left-of-center political institutions and journals that support a peace movement and are committed to a critical stance toward American economy and society. Lists of publications offered for sale typically include no systematic analyses of the operating characteristics of the war-making institutions of the United States. Neither do they highlight the problems of carrying out a reversal of an arms race, or of converting from military to civilian economy, or the possible relation between such planning and being able to reverse an arms race.

In a word, I find that American peace organizations have been characteristically oriented toward programs whose parts are not linked by a defined sequence of actions, or a theory, that might orient particular actions to a defined goal. An assortment of measures, each one of which is worthy in some limited sense, does not necessarily constitute, in combination, a movement toward diminishing the decision-power of the war-making institutions.

Peace organizations rarely attempt strategic planning. That means: defining long-term objectives and the programs of specific short-term actions that could sensibly lead to those goals. Again and again the people of the peace movement define their central role as that of *resisting* government policies. By forgoing the task of strategic planning, the peace movement positions itself primarily as a responder to government initiatives, leaving it to the war-making chiefs to set the agenda.

None of this is to say that response to government action is not essential. It is to say that the nature of response is strongly conditioned by the presence or absence of strategic planning and the presence or absence of political initiatives by peace organizations. Thus the resistance to the Vietnam war was not regularly accompanied by teachings that would have made the opposition part of a succession of moves designed to reduce the power of the war-making institutions. The lesson is plain: *a peace movement that confines itself to a progression of short-term resistance campaigns leaves political initiative to the warmakers by leaving the war-making institutions intact.*

With this posture *long-term goals like reversing the arms race, reducing the decision-power of the war-making institutions, planning for conversion from military to civilian economy, are displaced. Little or no attention is given to: how to move toward such goals from where we are now; which short-term actions are most serviceable for moving toward these goals.* It is not that a judgment is made that long-range goals are unachievable. The idea is hardly ever addressed. Instead, primary attention is given to organizing, financing, and administering bewildering varieties of short-term steps. These activities mobilize sizable money and human resources. They are used up in a kind of political meatgrinder, out of which there is little coordinate result in terms of movement toward long-term goals.

To illustrate. For about a month in 1985 I was beset with letters, flyers, special-delivery communications, and long-distance telephone calls to support the Great March from California, to become a faculty sponsor of studying to be done along the route from California to Washington, DC. A sum of money that exceeded the annual national budget of SANE was spent on efforts to organize an open-air march from coast to coast. The literature had a touch of magic: a march without a program except "peace"; no reference to war-making institutions and how the march might contribute to diminishing their power, no reference to economic conversion, no reference to disarmament as an international process to reverse the entire—not only nuclear—arms race.

(I should note that there are peace, and pro-peace, organizations that, like the American Friends Service Committee, are based upon strong personal, often religious, value commitments to peaceful, antiviolent behavior by individuals and governments. Such groups do have a long-term goal that is defined by the strong value-commitments of their members. But the focus of the present discussion is on political-economic institutional change, and that objective is not directly addressed by personal pacifist commitment.)

A major, unintended consequence of the conventional modes of activity by many US peace groups is to leave the war-making institutions, as institutions, virtually unchallenged. That is a consequence of an arms-control orientation toward regulating the behavior of those institutions and thereby contributes to keeping the war-making institutions intact, unchallenged. They are left to choose the initiatives, to which the peace organizations try to respond. As if lacking a separate identity, the peace organizations rarely initiate.

Witness what happens when peace groups do initiate—within the limits of short-termism. From coast to coast during

1984 ABC-TV broadcast the famous film "The Day After" on the nature of nuclear war. Millions were impressed with the vivid idea that nuclear war is different from anything they had previously understood as war-making. Peace organizations surely succeeded in channeling new fears of nuclear war toward support for the nuclear freeze movement. But the subsequent Republican and Democratic national political conventions paid no attention whatever to the idea of a nuclear weapons freeze. President Reagan dominated one convention with his plans for a military budget escalation, with buy-now, pay-later financing. Walter Mondale dominated the other convention with a similar military budget (actually a few percentage points less) and favored pay-as-you-go financing. So the two main political parties stood as one in support of the decision-power and material resources that should be given to the war-making institutions. President Reagan also captured a part of the "antinuclear" campaign by promising to save us from nuclear annihilation with his Strategic Defense Initiative umbrella.

Thereupon the freeze movement was left bewildered. Since all public opinion polls showed heavy majorities pro-freeze, how did this political defeat of the freeze campaign happen? A widely circulated "freeze" letter argued that the reason why the freeze was not advocated by either convention of the main parties (or by any principal platform speaker) was because the "experts" opposed it. Therefore, what was needed was a campaign to convince the "experts." Who, exactly, are the experts? They are the war planners, the theorists of the war-making institutions, the nuclear-strategy formulators, the shrewd political scientists, game theorists, and economists with theories of rational behavior who are prepared to counsel presidents on how to wield nuclear weapons for political leverage on opponents.

But advising a peace movement to try to convince the war-planning experts overlooks the identity of these people: they are the ideologues of the war-making institutions. A serious effort to alter the political judgment of these experts makes sense only within an arms-control framework that presumes sustained functioning and power of the war-making institutions. Plainly, those institutions have far more to offer these experts than does a peace movement—the continued value of their ideas (their intellectual capital), their jobs, money, status. Therefore it is futile and self-defeating for a peace movement to base any serious strategy on winning over these "experts."

SINGLE WEAPONS AS SINGLE ISSUES

Organizing around opposition to particular weapons has become a regular feature of many peace movement efforts. Consider the meaning of opposing nuclear weapons as a political target. Their destructiveness is not only real but gripping to the human imagination and therefore a natural rallying point. But the truth is also that the old-fashioned explosives and fire bombs that destroyed Hamburg, Dresden, and Tokyo did the same thing (minus the radioactive fallout, etc.). And nuclear weapons now overlap with nonnuclear weapons in their destructiveness. The US arsenal includes "fuel air" bombs with blast effect (1,000 lb./sq.in.) in a limited area like that of smaller nuclear weapons. Small nuclear weapons, with 100 tons of TNT equivalent and more, can be carried as "nuclear backpacks," or can be fired out of ordinary cannon, parts of the heavy artillery of traditional armed forces.

Unintended, one effect of a focus on antinuclearism is to invoke technological determinism, implying that the problem lies in the weapons, in the objects, not in the warmaking institutions that control their design, that fabricate them, justify them, write the manuals for their use, and train people in their use. Technological determinism deflects attention from the war-making institutions, from the command system that orders not only nuclear but every other kind of war as well.

Nuclear weapons are often opposed together with other

weapons of "mass destruction." How much lethality is "mass destruction"? Two people? Ten? A large family? A square block? A small town? A city? Does it have to be an entire country, a continent? Does particular opposition to weapons of "mass destruction" imply that the others are acceptable? The US armed forces are tooled up for a procession of wars of intervention in Central and Latin America and elsewhere. Nuclear weapons, the key weapons of "mass destruction," are not the preferred weapons for such wars. But their use is certainly not foreclosed as US armed forces are trained to apply winning strategies, and under some conditions state managers may decide that "winning" requires the use of nuclear weapons. (Note the rather different criterion for classifying weaponry that is part of the last [1962] US-USSR formulations of disarmament: residual national forces are internal police forces and their customary police equipment—ruling out all heavy weapons.)

An American peace movement must remember that the Pentagon's scientific, engineering, and industrial design departments—using one out of three engineers and scientists—can invent new weapons faster than a peace movement with modest resources can find out about them. A focus on single weapons as single issues is a losing strategy for a peace movement.

WHY DOES THE AMERICAN PEACE MOVEMENT HAVE THESE CHARACTERISTICS?

With few exceptions the organizations of the American peace movement have been oriented to arms-control patterns of narrow, short-term, single issues while leaning heavily on fear as a persuader. They have neglected, often avoided, direct address to reducing the power of the war-making institutions, and avoided planning sequences of initiatives aimed at achieving disarmament and economic conversion. Why?

I do not pretend to have *the* answer to this major problem. But I don't propose to duck the issue either.

Peace organizations function in a social environment that does not encourage long-range planning, democratic, participatory decision-making, the idea that society and economy can be seriously altered, and personal commitment to social goals that are not quickly attainable. Add to these discouragements the authoritarian managerial tradition that pervades most of the economic and related organizations in American life.

As long as peace organizations do not teach the political-institutional origin of establishment policies and avoid long-range planning, they act—intended or not—in accord with deeply rooted conventional wisdom. Also, political organizations that teach the background and significance of the main war/peace policy alternatives are less likely to be favored by financial and political support from arms-control institutions.

Many US peace organizations are headquartered in Washington, DC where proximity to the federal Executive and Congress invites close contacts between government and peace movement staffs in the pursuit of particular arms control moves.

The officers of peace groups have also developed a dependency on private foundations for funding parts of their activities. The influence of foundations has been visible not only in non-membership organizations, but also in bodies that have large dues-paying followings. There is, after all, a considerable administrative convenience in obtaining lumps of money in large single chunks as against many small bits of membership fees. But the policy consequences of this convenience have been far-reaching as peace organization officers and staffs trained themselves to think and plan in terms of "what are the funders interested in."

Foundation officers and trustees have, with rare exception, reflected the arms control orientation and preferences of the ruling establishment of American corporate and government institutions. Thereby, in the normal fashion, a multiplication of political influence has been achieved for short-term single-issue arms control methods and objectives. For every dollar of foundation grants it is prudent to assume that ten dollars worth of proposals have been received: hence that many more people are thinking about ways of formulating ideas, plans that will fit into the "programs" of the various foundations. As disarmament and economic conversion have not figured prominently, if at all, in those programs, the foundations have had sustained and ramified influence toward damping down innovative thinking, writing, teaching on economic conversion and disarmament.

Where leaderships see themselves as grand strategists seeking a succession of unlinked, single-issue arms-control successes, while guiding memberships with minor social commitment to the organization's goals, then there is pressure to rely on politically "safe" narrowly defined, short-term issues within a framework of appeal to nuclear fears. The best face of such a style is a form of political "pragmatism." It is also a political-organizational style that has been demonstrably vulnerable to government manipulation for deflecting serious threats to the political and economic hegemony of the war-making institutions. The ostensibly pragmatic, narrowly focussed, single-issue, nuclear-fearing peace-movement style is a political loser.

POLITICAL POWER AND THE ROLE OF IDEOLOGY

Peace organizations do not ordinarily address the nature of power, as in political life. Power does not consist merely of order-giving. Commands are of no consequence unless a population willingly accepts and willingly implements them. When a population says, "No," is unwilling to accept and to implement, then the power of decision-makers is checkmated. This is the recent lesson of Haiti and the Philippines.

The ability of the war-making institutions to get their orders implemented depends primarily on the willing compliance of the population. To be sure, the formal police and legal powers of the government are in place. These are competent to cope with small minority rejection of government authority. But the police powers cannot cope with overwhelming refusal to comply, to implement, to obey. That is why it is so important for the war-making managers to operate elaborate educational and media efforts to train the populace in ideology-belief systems that justify war-preparation and war-making.

The war-making institutions do not function autonomously. They contribute heavily to an environment of beliefs that sell their institutions. The selling of these beliefs takes place through the curricula, textbooks, and ceremonial rites of the schools (first grade through university) and through the mass media—print, radio, television.

What are these supporting beliefs? Three of them are the "master" beliefs. First, more armed forces mean more power, and military power can be made indefinitely large. (Accordingly, disarmament would spell powerlessness.) The second of these master beliefs is that "defense spending" boosts the economy. (Therefore, reducing military budgets would mean economic decline.) The third belief is that the war-making institutions provide protection against an evil, alien enemy. (Therefore, reversing the arms race means becoming vulnerable to pillage, enslavement.)

Subordinate to the master beliefs are a series of associated propositions. US resources are indefinitely large. Therefore it is possible to have guns and butter. Military force can therefore be used whenever and wherever the government of the United States wishes. Military spending not only boosts the national product, it adds to personal and national wealth. Military research and development and military technology are high tech, and therefore they boost the productiveness of civilian industrial and other activity. Finally, the United States is intrinsically, morally good and the USSR morally evil.

A common property of these statements is their mythic quality—visible as soon as the facts of the case are confronted. (See the Selected Readings on War Economy and Economic Consequences at the end of this volume.) However, with this array of beliefs, widely taught, widely accepted, the war-making institutions are solidly bolstered on every side.

Against the material, organizational, and ideological resources of the war-making institutions, consider the meaning of the peace supermarket. Even a chain of successes in narrowly focussed, short-term operations leaves the war-makers' ideological support system intact, or readily repaired—as following the US war in Vietnam.

If it is true that the decision-power of the nation's rulers relies crucially on popular allegiance, and if that allegiance is shored up by an ideological support system, then it is vital to know: how can the ideological support system of the war-making chiefs be overcome; where are they ideologically vulnerable?

To illustrate:

> The promise is for a guns and butter economy. The reality is lots of guns and decaying competence in civilian production and infrastructure, coupled with intensified exploitation—the rich getting richer and the poor more numerous.

> The promise is for a hi-tech based economy getting lots of spinoff from Star Wars and similar military projects. The reality is increasing dependence on imports for crucial electronic products and computer components, growing unreliability in fanciful military technologies, and accelerated depletion, especially in the civilian industrial economy.

> The promise is that boosting military budgets will yield more competent armed forces, more military power. The reality is that piling up more nuclear overkill is militarily meaningless, that the offense has overwhelming advantage among nuclear armed powers, and that there are definite limits to the competence of conventional forces as shown by the US performance in Vietnam and Lebanon.

The promise is that military spending can be readily used to bolster the economy. The reality is that money income and short-term employment can be boosted by almost any kind of spending. But sustained military spending has definite negative effects on productivity growth and thereby restricts every sort of production competence.

The promise is for "less government" and for economic "deregulation." The reality includes massive expansion of the Pentagon's management apparatus over military industry from 55,000 in 1970 to over 120,000 by 1985, intensification of managerial controls within the military economy, and over economic relations with other countries in the name of defense. At the same time there is real removal of federal constraints on dangerous working conditions in industry and on wealth accumulation by the super-rich.

The promise is to bolster the US as an opponent to totalitarian communism. The reality is that both the US and the USSR are societies with major internal economic class and ideological differences. Both societies boast "doves" and "hawks." The ideological furor in the US about the monolithic "evil empire" has the major effect—not of strengthening democratic institutions in the US—but of obscuring the divisions within each state, and the ways by which the hawks of each nation participate in a process of "antagonistic cooperation" by which the apparently hostile rulers of each society effectively bolster each other's internal power position.

A major weakness of the war-makers lies in the contradictions between the ideology that supports their system and reality. Hence it is a vital task of a peace movement to identify and explain those contradictions and to couple that with a specified plan, a road map, for deflating the warfare state and attaining peace.

For all that many people may wish to know a more comprehensive formulation of the condition of society without a war system. There was a time when the idea of socialism was a promise of a democratic, humane economic governance by a state that owned the means of production; and that organized their use and distributed their product by rules that tended toward democracy at the workplace, an abundance of output and egalitarianism in sharing the social product. The very existence of such an idea played a part in the long history of movements around the world that were critical of warmaking. For the partisans of peace could find there an ideological base that was an alternative to the capitalist status quo.

Be that as it may, that vision of an alternative to the exploitation and warmaking of capitalism was effectively nullified by the long tenure of Stalinism in the USSR, as Stalin spoke in the name of socialism while operating a totalitarian variant of state-controlled "command economy." And Adolph Hitler marched to power as chief of a "National Socialist German Workers Party." As an idea about an alternative to capitalism, socialism could not survive these assaults.

Independently of the validity of one or another part of this speculation, the fact is that in our time there is no widely accepted comprehensive grand theory of society in place of capitalism's variants. But that does not leave us without major political options. Workplace democracy is a serious alternative to managerial control. Its demonstrated workability and efficiency in the governance of modern industrial plants points to real possibility of combining democratic ways with high technology. At the same time, it is not unreasonable to expect that a diminution of managerialism as a system of decision-making in production, with its unlimited appetite for extension of control, will contribute toward damping down the urge to military power-wielding that has become so strong in both corporate and state managements.

The ideological displacement of the war system will also require a "moral equivalent of war," a set of social goals and ways of organizing for them that can evoke the excitement and political allegiance that had long been associated with politically popular military operations. Overcoming the warmaking institutions, organizing the great tasks of economic and other reconstruction, and inventing and developing related institutions of workplace democracy—all require social innovation on a large scale. The promise here is for the kind of excitement that gives purpose and meaning to living. I therefore judge that these goals have the potential for marshaling and holding the allegiance of men and women who seek a meaningful constructive and exciting lifestyle.

LINKING SPECIFIC ACTIONS TO LONG-TERM GOALS

The long-term goals of the peace movement are: disarmament —drastic reduction in the decision-power of the war-making institutions; conversion from military to civilian economy— the reassignment of the resources used for war-making to life-serving, constructive work.

These long-term goals each require a great array of specific actions organized along essentially two parallel tracks. One track is the political action for negotiated disarmament. The second track is legislation and allied action for planning and executing conversion from military to civilian economy.

The disarmament track. This requires an up-to-date blueprint of a draft treaty which peace organizations can press for negotiation by the US government. In April, 1962, the US government last proposed a comprehensive plan for reversing the arms race. A 1986 update prepared by Marcus Raskin and several colleagues is now in hand. The "Draft Treaty for a Comprehensive Program for Common Security and General Disarmament" should be studied inside the peace movement (see Selected Readings). Universities from coast to coast should be the scene of meetings and seminars explicating the significance of the blueprint for disarmament. Committees of the Congress should be urged to conduct formal, full-scale hearings on the blueprint for disarmament. Educating the media professionals is a crucial collateral task. Support for these moves by members and candidates for the Congress can be made a primary criterion for election support. All these actions can be oriented toward pressing for negotiation by the US government of such a treaty plan.

The economic conversion track. Since the economic conversion idea has advanced to the point where particular legislation has been proposed in the Congress, there is already a considerable fund of economic, industrial, and political background knowledge with respect to this policy. As noted earlier, the most recent legislative proposal in Congress is the economic conversion bill from Representative Ted Weiss (Dem., NY); it is a comprehensive plan for advance planning and execution of economic conversion in military-serving factories, laboratories, and bases. A considerable body of literature is available on the economic conversion idea (see Selected Readings).

A federal law is necessary for requiring the formation and operation of alternative-use committees at all important Pentagon-serving facilities, and for many of the other components of the Weiss conversion bill. At the same time there is vital work to be done on behalf of economic conversion in every city, state, and region. As indicated, capital investment plans for infrastructure repair in all these units will comprise a large set of new markets toward which conversion planners in firms and bases can be oriented.

The economic conversion issue is ready for wide dissemination as its legislative form has been thought through and represents the contribution of many interested parties. That is not to say that the (Weiss) bill cannot be improved. It is to say that concerned groups across the political spectrum will find that this proposal meets a serious requirement for preparing civilian economic opportunity in place of dependence on the military budget.

Support for the economic conversion bill. Hearings should be conducted in the relevant committees of both houses of Congress; wide support for this legislation should be sought among members of the House and the Senate; support should be solicited from candidates for public office and can be made a key criterion for election support. All these steps, with collateral education of media staffs, can be made into major parts of a national political effort, the very conduct of which would affect the tone of politics in the whole country. It is not unreasonable to expect that politicization of this quality will be accomplished as the peace movement arrays itself with related professional and political groups with a common stake in deflating the war-making institutions—economically and politically.

As against these perspectives, the peace movement has tended to misstate the problem. Once more, the arms-control-oriented groups have viewed themselves as active for peace while functioning as loyal, licensed critics of the war-making institutions. Others have sought out ways for seemingly easy wins, like combatting one weapons system at a time in national campaigns. On their face, those efforts have been seemingly all right as doing *something* to put a brake on some part of a military juggernaut. But this perspective has made it unnecessary to be in confrontation with the war-making institutions. Hence, inattention to either disarmament or economic conversion.

The disarmament proposal and the economic conversion plan can be made central issues for a North American peace movement—serving as long-term goals and guides for designing and executing short-term organizing and education operations in a multitude of spheres of life. These could include: new educational efforts on these topics in schools, community centers, political clubs; local, state, regional, and national coalitions with a common interest in diminishing the war-making institutions and converting the capital of military budgets to productive use; educating prospective candidates for public office; putting these issues onto the platform and floor at the conventions of the major political parties. The very conduct of a debate on these issues will alter the quality of national political discourse. It might even lead to elections with real choices!

The disarmament-plus-conversion orientation implies a set of political features: a grand strategy for moving away from the arms race and economic decay; a road map for politics that links short- and long-term actions; a way for the peace movement to set the political agenda. Further, it locates responsibility for the war system, contributes to a postmanagerial economy and society, and improves the security of the US and the quality of life for Americans.

For the many able and devoted organizers and governing committees in the peace movement this is a challenge beyond compare: to develop workable, innovative methods in every sphere of political education and organization; to maximize the political effectiveness of the resources at our disposal; to devise strategy and tactics to win.

The politics of peace as diagnosed here can be conducted as a two-track, parallel operation—treating disarmament and economic conversion. The selection of how and which one to stress at a given moment will be a function of the tactical situation. *What is most important is that a core question be constantly raised: what particular actions, among possible alternatives, will most fruitfully contribute to achieving these political goals?* This analysis implies that the selection of a particular concrete action should follow such a systematically repeated calculation.

It would be brash to assume that we could regularly make the most efficient choices. But it is sensible to expect a net gain in political effectiveness as we discipline ourselves to ask and answer these hard questions, every time.

The political strategy, short-term and long-term, that is defined here contains the prospect of coalition-building on the largest scale. *For the way is now open to demonstrate, credibly, that the normal workings of the war-making institutions checkmate every endeavor that is aimed at improving the human condition.* Against that miserable prospect the task of the peace movement is to show that there is an available, attractive alternative goal and a plan of action to get there.

The peace movement will gain political strengths as it trains its people not only in the economic imperatives but also in the moral advocacy that is appropriate to our legacy and our mission. We are bearers of the values of caring, life-serving community. We stand for the high worth of human life and are committed to converting the productive talents now wasted on war-making into economic resources applied to raising the quality of life. We propose disarmament for all states so that the crimes and destructiveness of war-making can be stopped and replaced by rules and institutions of law. For safeguarding these values and for their own sake we are strongly committed to democratic institutions and individual liberties.

These are the goals toward which the peace movement's road map should show the way.

4

Law for
Economic Conversion:
Necessity and Characteristics

There are two solid reasons for economic conversion planning: first, to facilitate reconstruction of the damage owing to a permanent war economy; second, to relieve disarmament negotiators of the fear that a reversal of the arms race carries unacceptable economic penalties.

On the face of it these considerations seem to be powerful, compelling. Hence, why are laws needed to require the necessary actions for these useful purposes?

Economic conversion law is required because major barriers must be overcome to set in motion the necessary planning process for reliable conversion operations. Managers in military industry, bases and laboratories fear a loss of power and privilege that would be caused by a reversal of the arms race and drastic reductions in military spending. Pentagon-serving managers have markets that are guaranteed by the federal government. They direct the production of goods and services that are sold before they are produced. The profitability of their operations is guaranteed by contract and tradition in the military economy. The top managers serving the Pentagon draw upon the finance capital capabilities of the entire society to facilitate their operations. Their proposals for weapons design and functions have far-reaching effects on both domestic and foreign policy of the United States government. These positions of power and privilege would indeed be diminished or eliminated if the arms race were reversed and military budgets reduced.

Why a *federal* law? The federal government alone is able to order economic conversion planning in the vast array of factories laboratories and bases that serve the Pentagon. Only the Washington, DC, government has the economic control over the military economy institutions as well as the clear legal power to order compliance with conversion procedures.

There is a further genuine fear among many of the people in military-serving industry, laboratories and bases: the expertise which they yield in the service of the military could become largely obsolete in the event of a major reduction in military requirements. It is normal for many men and women to regard a requirement for occupational retraining as fraught with personal and professional discomfort. Insofar as military-serving occupations have received higher pay and more rapid promotion than civilian-serving counterparts, the men and women in the service of the Pentagon often fear a reduction in income as well.

Finally, the whole society has been taught by economists, from right to left, that military goods and services are a source of wealth—like anything else with a price tag. Propelled by this myth, there is a fear that reduction in military spending could entail a loss of both employment and wealth.

Accordingly, there are no grounds for expecting that the managers of military economy would, on their own, set in motion the competent planning process that is required for moving from military to civilian work. For these reasons law is needed to make the necessary action mandatory, to compel the actions that are in the economic and political interests of the larger society.

The following are ten major components of law for facilitating economic conversion planning and operations.

1. *Mandatory alternative use committees.* Every military-serving factory, laboratory and base above a given size—say, 100 employees—should be required to establish, as a condition of its military service, an alternative use committee with responsibility for preparing blueprint-ready plans for civilian work in the

event that the military service of the people and facilities is no longer required. This committee is best composed—equally—of representatives of management and the working people, all occupations. This sharing of responsibility and authority is designed to assure not only a maximum flow of ideas, but also responsibility to both the administrators and to the working people of a factory, laboratory or base. The alternative use committee must be guaranteed access to whatever data and facilities it requires for fulfilling this function. The availability of alternative use plans, reviewed periodically—say, every two years—assures the people of the military-serving facility that competent attention has been given to their economic prospects beyond the service of the military.

I underscore that this need for alternative use committees, and the following features of conversion planning, pertain to university-based military research as well.

2. *Advanced conversion planning.* Planning for economic conversion can not be left to be set in motion at the time when say, a military contract, has been cancelled or quantities seriously reduced. The basic reason is the time period required for planning alternative use of buildings, equipment and people. There is no simple formula for making a competent selection of new products for a military-serving facility. Careful attention must be given not only to market requirements but also to the suitability of people and equipment for prospective new work. Beyond product selection there are the further tasks of refashioning machinery and production layouts; investigating new materials and arranging for sources of supply; and pre-testing materials, equipment and whole processes prior to new production operations. A period

of two years is a reasonable time allotment for these functions.

3. *Advanced notification of contract termination.* Government top managers must be required to give reasonable notification, say a year in advance, to factories, laboratories and bases when major projects are to be terminated. Such advanced notification is essential for facilitating orderly changeover and avoiding chaotic conditions and crash programs.

4. *Mandatory occupational retraining.* Professional retraining is a particularly important matter for the managerial and engineering-technical occupations. Managers have become highly specialized, as required by the particular rules and modes of operation suitable for the service of the military. Thus, a marketing manager who has been long experienced in the service of the military is skilled in the political-diplomatic requirements of that vocation, differing considerably from the skill necessary for selling to civilian department stores. Engineers who have become skilled in design and related operations that are carried out with indifference to cost must be fundamentally reoriented to the design problems that must be solved where cost minimizing and civilian reliability requirements dominate the scene. For these reasons, occupational retraining for administrators and engineers who have been long in the service of the military must be made mandatory as a part of economic conversion law. Available evidence indicates that only a minority of production workers may be so specialized in their occupational skills as to require retraining for suitability to civilian work.

5. *Community economic adjustment planning.* Where

military-serving industry, laboratories and bases are present in significant clusters, then the characteristics of entire communities are subject to major reshaping as part of economic conversion. For example, conversion to civilian work of many industrial facilities will entail a significant reduction in the number of engineering-technical people required, or a major movement in and out of the community of these occupations. In either event, major costs are entailed for the communities involved. Accordingly, planning funds should be made available for blue-printing the necessary adjustment operations.

6. *Decentralized control of alternative use planning.* There is no standardized formula or blueprint that can be universally applied for economic conversion planning. The work must be done with attention to the requirements of specific products and the capabilities and limitations of particular work forces, plant and equipment, surrounding infrastructure and resources. Accordingly, the operation of alternative use committees and related activity for conversion planning is most effectively carried out at the point of operation of the facilities concerned. This does not, in any way, detract from the feasibility or importance of calling upon specialized skills from any other place to facilitate the work in hand. But this does emphasize that a remotely positioned centralized organization is emphatically unsuited for economic conversion planning.

7. *Income maintenance during civilian conversion.* Even with blueprint-ready plans and schedules in hand there is no avoiding the prospect of a changeover period from military to civilian work. Under the best conditions months are required to set in motion even the best prepared plans. Moreover, it is prudent to under-

stand that time is needed for discovery of error and correction. Accordingly, preparation for economic conversion should provide for income maintenance to the people involved. This can be done by rules that are socially validated by previous practice. For example, in the US auto industry the combination of unemployment insurance and income support systems agreed by management and the unions have provided for as much as 90 percent of previous pay during a period of scheduled unemployment. Such provisions do not preclude the use of unemployment time as professional training and upgrading time.

8. *Relocation allowances.* Military-serving industrial units are often overloaded with administrative and engineering-technical people. Therefore, major industrial and geographic relocation is to be expected as part of conversion to civilian economy. The moving expenses for entire households can be substantial and should be an integral part of economic conversion law.

9. *A national network for employment opportunity.* Precisely because of the predictable requirement for major relocation of engineers, administrators and many production workers, a sensible part of economic conversion planning should be provision for a national network for employment opportunity. This will be especially important to production workers of those facilities that are not readily convertible to civilian use. This must be expected for the more exotic military-related operations, e.g., remotely located facilities for testing warheads and rocket engines, and the production and stockpiling of unusually volatile and dangerous munitions. It is therefore reasonable to expect that concentrations of need for new employment sites will be a characteristic condition of military-civilian con-

version. A national employment network should help to solve this problem.

10. *Capital investment planning by government.* The operation of a large military economy for more than forty years has entailed major underinvestment in the facilities and services called infrastructure. These are the roads, water systems, waste disposal operations, education plant and work forces, libraries, public health operations, parks, communication and transportation systems, etc., etc. Neglect of these facilities and their staffs typically requires large capital investments. Detailed planning for these purposes by the local and national government bodies that are responsible for infrastructure facilities and operations will make a major contribution to competent conversion planning. For the large markets that are opened up by infrastructure maintenance and renewal are part of the alternative product system towards which many military-industry firms, laboratories, and bases can be reoriented. Hence, capital investment plans by governments at all levels will comprise a major contribution toward defining new markets and jobs for converting factories, laboratories, and bases.

There is a further characteristic of economic conversion law that can have a major effect. That pertains to the location of the national economic conversion commission, or similar body within a national government. To many of the people connected with one or another aspect of military economy, the prospect of conversion planning suggests that it be located within the very agency that is responsible for administering the existing military economy. In the United States this would mean assigning major administrative responsibility for conversion operations to the Department of Defense. Indeed, this seems to be a prudent way to address these problems in the eyes of many lawmakers and others who have had long careers developing liaison with the Pentagon in the service of local military industry, research, and base operations. The elemental logic of these people comes down to this: why not locate responsibility for conversion to civilian work precisely in the place that organizes all the military-serving work.

Alas, this apparent convenience also entails strengthening the decision power of the war-making institutions, and the prospect of continuing the criteria of decision-making and methods of operation that have become characteristic of permanent military economies. These methods are precisely unsuited to the civilian economy. Indifference to cost and product reliability assures incompetence and failure in the civilian sphere. Also, continuity of style of working is bolstered by continuity of organization. Hence reshuffling people and responsibilities is a necessary part of assuring a change, a conversion, from military to civilian methods of working. Indeed, if responsibility and authority for administering economic conversion planning and operations were to be vested in the directorate of military economy, that would be tantamount to creating a Ministry of National Economy with ways of working involving, effectively, an enlargement of military economy rather than a conversion.

A vital feature of economic conversion law is the absence of subsidies to the managers of converting enterprises. Subsidies in the form of guarantees of capital, or markets, or profitability would tend to reinforce cost-maximizing and the accompanying ways of inefficiency and incompetence—that are precisely the obverse of the requirements for competent conversion of civilian economy.

The implementation of these characteristics of economic conversion law may be facilitated or made more difficult by one or another surrounding condition of economy, politics, or ideology. However, the essential law requirements for competent economic conversion are specific to the common characteristics of modern military economy, wherever located.

The specifications discussed here for desirable components of economic conversion law are fulfilled in H.R.813, a proposed law initiated in the House of Representatives of the United States Congress on January 28, 1987 by congressman Ted Weiss (Dem., N.Y.).

Because of the long duration and power of military economy, a considerable body of ideology has been built up, not only justifying its functioning but also offering reasons why economic conversion planning is unnecessary, unrealistic, or both. Here are some of the key ideas in this realm.

Ideology. First there must be political agreement to scale down the war system. Then conversion to civilian economy can be taken care of. *Reality.* Industrial planning experiments have shown that two years is a necessary planning time for a factory of, say, one to two thousand employees. Therefore advance preparation is necessary to avoid economic chaos when military production is completely stopped—as it must be to assure compliance with a reversal of the arms race.

Ideology. The reconversion of US and Soviet war industry at the end of World War II showed that turning to civilian work is no problem. *Reality.* At the close of World War II US and Soviet military factories reconverted to products and methods they had known and used before the war. The present military economies around the world are typically composed of facilities that are specialized for the military work, hence a conversion, not a reconversion, problem.

Ideology. In market-driven economies conversion to civilian economy can be left to market forces. *Reality.* The anticipated hardships of a "free market" conversion adjustment is one of the political factors that locks the military-serving labor force into fear-driven political actions for sustaining military economy, and hence the arms race.

Ideology. In centrally planned economies the state planning committees (like Gosplan) can do the necessary planning when the problem arises. *Reality.* The Gosplan-type central planning methods are now understood as barriers to economic development in the USSR and—efficient or not—central planning agencies do not eliminate the need for advance planning at the point of production for economic conversion.

Ideology. Economic conversion planning should be left to the large corps of able managers and engineers already in place in military industry and other facilities. *Reality.* The managers and engineers of military industry are trained to maximize cost and maximize subsidies from the state. These practices guarantee failure in designing and producing civilian products and services. That is why occupational retraining is a mandatory part of the Weiss conversion bill.

Ideology. Military industry can simply be given orders for new civilian products by the government. *Reality.* Top managers and engineers in military industry would welcome a continuation of government subsidy, thereby ensuring their power and privilege. But this would also guarantee gross inefficiency in the performance of the civilian work.

Ideology. Existing organizations of military industry under ministries of defense can be readily utilized for assigning new, civilian product work. *Reality.* By such methods a ministry of defense is changed into a virtual ministry of the national economy, also ensuring that the institutionalized inefficiencies of military industry will be applied to an ever-wider economic sphere.

Ideology. Whether done by a ministry of defense or a separate agency, economic conversion must be nationally centralized and coordinated. *Reality.* Efficient conversion planning requires the sort of detailed, specific knowledge typically available only among the people engaged at particular industrial, military base and other facilities. Remote control is the incompetent way for carrying out detailed planning operations.

Ideology. Economic conversion can be readily carried out by the top managements of enterprises that are skilled in diversification techniques. *Reality.* Product, market, and investment diversification can be financially effective for enterprises as a whole, but that does not cope with the specific material problems for planning the retraining and redesign of manufacturing facilities and the work forces involved.

Ideology. The conversion perspective ignores the idea of military industry as a prime source of new technology. *Reality.* Military economy is indeed a prime source of military technology, which has become, worldwide, increasingly specialized and remote from civilian requirements.

Ideology. Economic conversion is primarily a problem for the nuclear superpowers. *Reality.* Every modern military budget is an equivalent capital fund that sets in motion the resources ordinarily understood as fixed and working capital. Therefore, every modern military budget represents a sum of capital goods and services foregone from civilian economic development.

Ideology. Since influential power-wielders in every government have a stake in the continuation of military economy, the economic conversion idea is simply wishful thinking. *Reality.* No government wishes to preside over a second, let alone a third-rate, economy. In both industrialized and developing economies the contradiction between economic development and military economy is inescapable and, characteristically, ever more intense. This generates a conflict from which there is only one constructive solution for the overwhelming majority of society: economic conversion planning and accompanying reversal of the arms races.

Ideology. The economic conversion idea ignores the fact that military economy adds to the nation's wealth by adding to the money-valued national product. *Reality.* It is true that military goods and services are given money value, but it is also the fact that these goods and services are not useful for ordinary consumption or as means of production. This restriction on the use-value of the products of military economy is the source of the contradiction between military economy and economic development.

5
Strategic Factors for Designing a Disarmament Process

Disarmament is a process for diminishing the power of war-making institutions by mutual agreement among governments. Mutual agreement on military, political, and economic matters must include, crucially, agreements for carefully phased and inspected reduction of armed forces, weapons, budgets, as well as military-serving factories, laboratories, bases, and the number of people—civilian and uniformed—under their control.

More than a definition of disarmament is needed at this point in our narrative. For Americans educated in the high schools and universities of the United States from 1963 to 1988 were not informed about the idea of disarmament. If mentioned at all, then it was treated as a visionary ideal, at best and, at worst, a device for leaving the United States helpless, without weapons in the face of Soviet threat. Most important perhaps, what was wiped out during the quarter century 1963–1988 was the fact that the government of the United States, in the person of President Kennedy, had formally presented plans for carrying out a reversal of the arms race, and that this had been done in concert with the Soviets. That history was simply withdrawn from public discussion; after the Orwellian fashion of *1984*, put down the memory hole.

While the expansion of Department of Defense budgets dominated the activity of President Kennedy's first year in office, there were also initiatives in other directions. With strong encouragement and support from Jerome Wiesner, his science adviser, and leading members of the Senate (notably Hubert Humphrey and Joseph Clark), President Kennedy supported legislation establishing an Arms Control and Disarmament Agency in the State Department. To chair the advisory committee of that agency Kennedy appointed John J. McCloy, then recently retired as president of the Chase Bank in New York City. McCloy took this post very seriously, and proceeded to address banking and other business groups from coast to coast arguing the importance of peace and disarmament on economic, moral and political grounds.

During 1961, in order to explore the international terrain with respect to disarmament, McCloy engaged in a series of discussions with Valerian Zorin, the Soviet chief delegate to the United Nations. Following six meetings in the United States and Europe, these men formulated a three-page text comprising a set of criteria, principles to which detailed disarmament plans by the United States and Soviet governments should conform. This short text was announced with much fanfare and was unanimously adopted by the General Assembly of the United Nations. Thereafter, senior government staffs in both the United States and the Soviet Union proceeded to formulate disarmament plans.

The United States disarmament plan was announced in April 1962 by President Kennedy. The proposal bore the title "Blueprint for the Peace Race: The United States Plan for General and Complete Disarmament in a Peaceful World." The Soviet disarmament plan was formally presented in September 1962.

But the Cuban Missile Crisis of October 1962 put an end to serious negotiation on the US and Soviet disarmament proposals. The Soviet high command emerged from that crisis with determination never to be caught again in the same position of gross military inferiority. On the American side, the dominant view in the White House staff was one of exhiliration: they had learned how to play nuclear chicken and win. Thereafter, the Cuban Missile Crisis was celebrated by mainstream American political and military strategy analysts as a crowning and model achievement in the wielding of nuclear military power for political effect. (In my judgement the conventional American view of the Cuban Missile Crisis has played an important formative role for both strategy specialists and a wider public. I have, therefore, added an epilogue to this book on the Cuban Missile Crisis as this presents an explanation of the Missile Crisis events altogether different from the conventional wisdom of American academic analysts.)

Against this background, arms control strategy dominated the field. The arms race was to be made into a managed, regulated activity, to the exclusion of disarmament.

Twenty-Five Years of Blackout on Disarmament

Soon after the Kennedy administration was established in 1961, concerted efforts were launched by departments of the government, by the major private foundations, by principal universities—all to the point of establishing arms control, the regulation of the arms race, as the primary orientation for wielding American military/political power—all this at the side of strategic studies with their classic emphasis on superiority in military/political operations.

The Ford and Rockefeller Foundations, which together have accounted for about 85 percent of international relations research grants at American universities, set in motion elaborate programs of arms control activities: institutes, seminars, conferences, research grants, journals. The word was out in the universities: graduate students and university faculties could immediately see where money was to be had for graduate work in international affairs. Each of the two lists below—1987–88 Grants for Research and Teaching awarded by the University of California's Institute on Global Conflict and Cooperation, and IGCC 1987 Seminar Presentation Topics—is a case in point.

Institute on Global Conflict and Cooperation of the University of California: Research/Teaching Grants Awarded 1987–88

The Discourse of the Nuclear Arms Debate
Learning from History in US Foreign Policy: The Case of the Middle East
Conflicts Surrounding the South Pacific Nuclear Free Zone Treaty: Implications for US Policy in the South Pacific
Successes and Failures: Goals, Methods, and Outcomes in Anti-Nuclear War Efforts
Domestic Determinants of Arms Races and Arms Control: US-Soviet Comparative Analysis
Strategic Language: A Literary Analysis of Deterrence Discourse
Crisis Management: Structural Syncretisms of the International, Group, Interpersonal, and Intrapsychic Levels
Superpower Rivalry and Political Instability in the Third World: Dilemmas for American Foreign Policy
The Expansion of Sovereignty: Conflict Management and the Constitutive Principle in International Relations
Moral Vision and Foreign Policy: The Case of US-China Relations
China and the Sea: Economic, Security and Domestic Political Implications
Political Economy of Defense Spending
George Kennan and the Dilemmas of US Foreign Policy
The Purge of Fang Li Zhi: The Tension Between Science and Ideology in Contemporary China
The Arms Race in the News Media; and, Course Preparation on Nuclear Age Culture and Discourse
Silicon Valley Research Group/ORA in High Technology and Social Change

IGCC *1987 Seminar Presentation Topics*

History of the Arms Race
History of Arms Control
Deterrence Theory
Environmental Consequences of Nuclear War
Causes of War
How a Nuclear War Might Start
Soviet Decision-Making for National Security
Soviet Views on Arms Control
US Decision-Making for National Security
Panel: Negotiating with the Soviets
Current Arms Control Negotiations and Their
  Consequences
The Role of Congress and Congressional Staff in National
  Security Issues
Panel: Alliance Relations and European Security
Fear of Cheating, Fear of Spying
US Defense Spending
Arms Control without Negotiation: The Role of Unilateral/
  Independent Initiatives
Psychology of the Arms Race
Ethical and Moral Issues of the Arms Race
US-USSR Seismographic Cooperation
Chemical and Biological Warfare
The European Peace Movement
Nuclear Non-Proliferation.

The arms control emphasis by the foundations and the universities was, of course, strongly supported and politically validated by the participation of senior members of the government in arms control and arms control-related activities.

As for disarmament: no research grants at all from the major foundations; no research grants at all from the US Arms Control and Disarmament Agency; no courses at universities; no doctoral dissertations leading to degrees on disarmament topics; no treatment of disarmament topics in major journals of opinion. For twenty-five years, major publishers did not produce a single book on disarmament authored by an American writer.

During the twenty-five year blackout on disarmament a new generation of specialists in political science, international affairs, journalism, and kindred fields was trained by American universities with the understanding that disarmament was a concept devoid of serious political relevance: without doubt an arcane visionary idea attributable only to devout pacifists or political cultists. Disarmament was redefined to mean unilateral reduction or abandonment of armed force, rather than a mutually agreed, mutually advantageous process of arms race reversal. In that context the Cold War and its arms race are forever, irreversible.

Some graduate courses in political science made passing mention of the McCloy-Zorin agreements with one lecturer describing that as a public relations ploy by the Kennedy administration. As to President Kennedy's disarmament plan: it has been dealt with by not being referred to at all; or if mentioned, then designated too as a public relations ploy.

At this writing, in 1988, I am pleased to report that recent research done by Robert Krinsky in the Kennedy archives has uncovered previously classified White House internal documents in which President Kennedy set forth his precise attitudes and policy formulations concerning disarmament and the arms race. The publication of these documents, including those written after the Cuban Missile Crisis, will correct the distortions invented by the arms control and strategic policy intellectuals.

By 1988 the blackout on the idea of reversing the arms race is being ended. After forty years of arms race and Cold War, parts of the ruling elites of the United States and the Soviet Union confronted their internal economic condition and found that grave problems could not be addressed without damping down and reversing the arms race. The idea of disarmament could no longer be kept under wraps. The very onset of the US Senate debate on the Intermediate Nuclear Force Treaty set in motion a discussion that called attention to the merits and limitations of this treaty, not only within a narrow compass, but also in light of possible future agreements—as on intercontinental ballistic missiles and with respect to conventional forces. That discussion compelled attention to the merits of formulating an orderly process for carrying out a reversal of the arms race, all aspects. In order to do that a series of problems that are intrinsic to a disarmament process must be addressed.

PROBLEMS OF DESIGNING A DISARMAMENT PROCESS

Since 1962 virtually no attention has been given to the problems of designing, negotiating, and implementing a disarmament process in the principal countries of the world. Moreover, since that time the technical, political, and economic problems entailed in reversing the arms race have been complicated by the great enlargement of armed forces, the stockpiles of their weapons, the size of their budgets and of supporting manufacturing and scientific establishments. Accordingly, it is vitally important to give fresh attention to the array of problems whose solution is essential for confidence in designing and implementing a disarmament process.

I start from the assumption that mutual assurance for carrying out a disarmament process for common security cannot be achieved on the basis of vaguely defined mutual trust. Reliable inspection methods are needed to verify compliance with the terms of a disarmament process.

In the ordinary conduct of our lives, we rely on compliance with a great array of agreements on codes of behavior whose violation is commonly viewed as unthinkable, even apart from the presence of law-enforcing institutions. A special problem surrounding a disarmament process is that its subject is a network of war-making institutions whose operators have a long tradition and extensive training in secrecy, deception, surprise, and evasion—the better to overcome the opponent. These ordinary, thinkable and valued aspects of military institutions, together with the many millions of people who participate in them, tell us that the design and execution of a disarmament process must give elaborate attention to workable and reliable ways of ensuring compliance by the participating states. This will require multiple barriers against successful evasion of the terms of a disarmament agreement. That assessment derives not from a paranoid, unreasonably exaggerated view of armed forces and their supporting organizations, but rather from sober and prudent understanding of the quantity and quality of resources that have been made available to secret intelligence and military organizations trained to carry out covert military, political, industrial and research operations on a large scale.

The following problems are formulated to invite fresh and many-sided approaches to their solution.

Since national armed forces are not symmetrical, how should weapons and manpower be categorized for counting them and carrying out a reduction process? US armed forces have more aircraft carriers than the Soviets and fewer tanks. The Soviets have more ships in their navy, but the US navy is composed of much larger ships. How should one count military manpower? If civilians are employed to do housekeeping at military bases or elsewhere for armed forces, should they be counted as military personnel? Sophisticated weapons and their auxiliary equipments require major maintenance facilities. If these are manned in part by civilians, should they be counted as part of military personnel?

If a mutually agreed reduction of armed forces is to be carried out, a set of categories must be developed for classifying and counting military personnel and military materiel with as few "loose ends" as possible. Furthermore, since armed forces are not symmetrical among countries, it is unreasonable to expect that a set of categories could be developed and applied to make the effects of weapons and forces reduction equal in all respects.

For example, a 10 percent reduction in naval forces could be based upon alternative possible categories, as follows: naval vessels, all classes, including training and support; tonnage of naval vessels, all classes, including training and support.

The military-political significance of the selection of categories for 10 percent reduction will be affected by the array of missions for which the navies have been designed. Accordingly, there is merit in preferring categories which, at once, yield a real reduction in material and forces while also permitting the exercise of choice by military-political commanders with respect to maximizing the military-political potential of residual forces at each step in a disarmament process. I judge that the built in ability to make such choices as part of a disarmament process will give more confidence in the process as a transition system toward non-military based institutions for national security.

The following are a set of categories for classifying and counting armed forces and personnel that are designed to meet the requirements just discussed.

Tonnage of naval vessels, all classes.
Number of ground vehicles for launching munitions
    < 5 mile range.
Number of ground vehicles for launching munitions
    > 5 mile range.
Number of all other powered ground vehicles.
Number of airborne vehicles for delivering munitions
    < 300 mile range.
Number of airborne vehicles for delivering munitions
    > 300 mile range.
Number of all other airborne vehicles.
Tons of munitions and launchers, personnel-carried.
Tons of munitions, all other.
Number of nuclear warheads < 10 kt.
Number of nuclear warheads > 10 kt.
Number of persons in military formations and bases.

At what rate should weapons and forces be reduced? Should the rate of reduction be rapid enough to persuade all parties that a significant reversal process is really in motion, while slow enough to forestall political panic? Military as well as political considerations are involved here. Consider that for purposes of offensive military planning advantages in the ratio of three to one and more are customarily desired. In that context, reductions of armed forces of, say, 10 percent cannot appear to be militarily significant. However, a succession of 10 percent reductions has major effect in due course.

How should production of military materiel be dealt with? Should production be stopped completely at an agreed date? Or, should production of weapons and "maintenance" spare parts be gradually phased out? These are vital considerations because of the size of the industrial and scientific establishments that support armed forces in principal countries. Thousands of factories and hundreds of laboratories are involved. Immediately, this implies the problem of inspection and verification of permitted behavior.

From the standpoint of optimum reliability of an inspection system the most desirable condition is complete cutoff of research and production of military materiel by a given date. The starting date should be the first day on which the disarmament process comes into force. That would mean that the period of negotiation plus any subsequent agreed interregnum until starting Day 1 would be a time during which each participant country could produce military materiel, including spare parts, at will. On Day 1 of the disarmament process, all this should halt. Under this procedure it is possible to put in place and operate a highly reliable system of inspection and verification of the halt in research and production. Thus the closing of a factory, or its conversion to civilian products is easily confirmed. By contrast, continued development and production of whole weapons, or production of components for maintenance purposes, introduces complicated problems. Thus when the production of military components is part of the work of a machine shop it can be very difficult to trace and confirm the particular military-specific components. Very often a machinist does not necessarily know the planned end use of a workpiece for the production of which he carries out only a fraction of the total number of required operations. Under such conditions opportunities for evasion and deception are multiplied.

The clear advantage for reliability of a disarmament process is on the side of a complete cessation of production of military materiel and components. Such a halt would not pertain to non-military-specific "housekeeping" types of goods and services like food, fuel, and clothing. For the rest, the maintenance and continued workability of the gradually diminished armed forces would have to be served out of stores of materiel accumulated and left in place at the beginning of the disarmament process.

What are strategic problems of inspection for verification under conditions of reversing an arms race, as differentiated from the inspection problems that are to be expected under arms control agreements? Arms control agreements are designed to set limits to specific aspects of the arms race and thereby to regulate them. This means that an arms control scenario includes continuation of the normal and powerfully impelled drive among military organizations to seek ways for achieving military superiority. Also, since arms control agreements are oriented narrowly, to particular weapons for example, such agreements leave the largest part of military organizations intact—with their trained capacity for deception and evasion. By contrast, disarmament involves definite reductions in armed forces and their weapons, across the board. Within the framework of a disarmament treaty, government leaders confront the prospect of diminished military institutions and less reliance on the national armed forces for common security.

These differences have major consequences for the conduct and reliability of inspection operations. Under arms control scenarios all the traditional military institutional drives for seeking advantage through deception, evasion, secrecy, qualitative changes in weaponry, and numerical advantage are present in full force. In the disarmament perspective, the influence of these considerations is necessarily abridged by the predictable pattern of diminished numbers of forces and weapons. For example, in the arms control scenario, military research proceeds full tilt in the search for technical advantages, while in a disarmament scenario such perspectives are constrained by the termination of military research and production.

What are the capabilities and limitations of physical inspection of military economies and armed forces? An agreement for termination of military production could be verified with high reliability. Inspection methods could range from single persons posted at former military industry sites to the use of remote-controlled television cameras for monitoring entrances, exits, and interiors of former military production sites. For military industry locations that are converted to civilian work, inspection and verification of the new activity can be readily carried out to confirm the revised products and allied production systems.

The long duration of military economy has given rise to a super problem in the form of the large sizes and diversity of location of military inventories. I take as my base line the condition of armed forces and military economies in 1958 when the first comprehensive investigation of inspection for disarmament was carried out (see Melman, *Inspection for Disarmament*). At that time large scale production of missiles was hypothesized but had not yet occurred. Since then military economy and armed forces have undergone major expansion, missiles of all types and sizes are being mass-produced, and techniques for secrecy and evasion have been elaborated. The latter were made more dangerous for a disarming process owing to the multiplication in the number and resources of intelligence and covert operations organizations in the principal countries of the world.

Physical inspection of armed forces is facilitated by their concentration on a limited number of bases and other centers.

But the armed forces of the United States, the Soviet Union, the NATO countries of Western Europe, China, and India are now so large—with hundreds of bases in each case—as to automatically complicate the inspection problem. Should it be an essential part of a disarmament agreement to require a consolidation of armed forces on fewer bases and similar sites? A diminished number of military bases can be, in its own right, an important contribution toward lessening capability for evasion of a disarmament treaty.

What are the strengths and weaknesses of the geographic type of zone inspection system that was formulated about twenty-five years ago? The idea of doing detailed inspection of armed forces during a disarmament process on a geographic zone basis represents an accommodation to two kinds of conditions: first, the enormous size of armed forces, making it difficult to do other than detailed inspection and verification of geographically sampled parts of the system in any one limited time period; second, this is an accommodation to the normal and powerful military penchant for secrecy. The latter is accommodated by doing a complete checkout of the inventory of armed forces and weaponry in place in only part of a country during a given phase of the disarmament process.

Should military research and development be permitted during a disarmament process? If not, how can reduction/termination be reasonably assured? Prudence dictates termination of military R&D in parallel with halting weapons production. Where military R&D requires uniquely specialized facilities, like remotely sited rocket testing facilities or very large wind tunnels, the closing or conversion of these facilities to civilian use could be verified in fairly straightforward fashion. It is also significant that large parts of military-related research pertain to product design, field-testing and evaluation of military products. This requires large field-testing facilities and major technical staffs focussing on aspects of product development. This too lends itself readily to inspection and verification as, for example, test areas for armored warfare vehicles. However, important parts of military related R&D can be carried out with equipment, facilities, and people similar to those required for many classes of civilian research. In that case, what goes on in people's minds plays a crucial role, and that is a major limit on physical inspection capability! Furthermore, that is precisely the reason for considering the following problem.

What methods, apart from physical inspection techniques, can be used to reinforce the reliability of inspection for disarmament? It was out of respect for the possibilities of evasion techniques, especially in the hands of technically trained people, that the idea of "inspection by the people" was developed for the study on *Inspection for Disarmament* in 1958. Our judgement at that time was that it is essential to mobilize the active participation of large populations in support of the disarmament process. In particular, we judged it necessary, as a formal part of a treaty on disarmament to require the chief of state of each signatory government to address their own population to educate and persuade them in the idea that they must, as an obligation of citizenship, report to an international disarmament inspectorate any evidence of behavior that may be in violation of the treaty. This idea, and the development of techniques to ensure its reliable functioning, is indispensable for the purpose of curbing possible evasion of a disarmament treaty. Studies of the methods used for organizing and operating secret military production and secret military formations show that many people acting together would be required for militarily and politically significant evasion of a disarmament process. That is a vulnerability which can be utilized by an alert citizenry acting in support of a disarmament process.

What are the strategic factors appropriate for the design and operation of an international inspectorate with responsibility for ensuring compliance with a disarmament treaty? No one will dispute the idea that such an international inspectorate must be truly multinational. That requirement would have to be met while high standards of selection and staff performance are enforced. For an International Disarmament Organization, in the nature of its functioning, must have a very low tolerance for incompetence.

Apart from the operational staff, it will be vital to have policy-making bodies of the international inspectorate composed of representatives from the participating countries in order to assure mutual confidence in the basic policies of such an agency. The staff participants in an international inspection organization will have to be given unique rights of citizenship including the right to live in any country of their choice upon completion of their obligations to the inspectorate. The people of the inspectorate will have to be given special status as an elite community in the service of all mankind. After serving specified periods of time in the international organization these men and women will also have to be assured minimum livelihood thereafter.

Also, an array of legal issues, varying among countries, are raised by the prospect of an international inspectorate that requires extraordinary access to people and places (factories, offices, laboratories, homes, files, letters, etc.) in the course of verifying compliance with and countering evasion of a disarmament process. (See the works by L. Henkin, D. Aronowitz, and H. J. Berman and P. B. Maggs in the Selected Readings.)

Assuming that a disarmament agreement is initiated by the us-ussr, *how are other states to be brought into the process?* It will be in the self-interest of the governments of the United States and the Soviet Union to see to it that all the nations that are allied to each of them join in the international disarmament agreement. The economic, political, and military power that would be represented by these groupings of states would have a combined weight so great as to persuade any other nation in the world as to the prudence of joining in a worldwide consortium for disarmament. The terms of the disarmament treaty and the mode of operation of an international disarmament organization must furthermore provide for participation by the increased number of states joining in the process.

What problems may be anticipated in the design of international peacekeeping forces that would be required as part of international institutions for conflict resolution built up in parallel with a disarmament process? Innovative methods will have to be developed for the design and operation of international military forces. For example, under United Nations auspices military peacekeeping forces have been established following debate and decision by the General Assembly, the Security Council, or both. However, a peacekeeping force set up in parallel with a disarmament treaty may be required to operate in such a way as to give high assurance, especially to smaller states, that this international force is always and swiftly available to safeguard them. Thus, the dispatch of the international peacekeeping force to the site of an alleged border violation could be carried out, automatically, upon the receipt of a complaint from a member government. Thereby, the international peacekeeping military unit would operate in the fashion of a big city fire department or police force which responds speedily to a declared emergency without any required consultation with the mayor, or the city legislative body.

The operation of an international peacekeeping force would also have to be linked to the functioning of an international judicial system for receiving and resolving disputes among states under rules that require speedy referral of disputes by the international military force for adjudication. In establishing such institutions the major governments of the world would carry a responsibility for demonstrating by example their support for such new arrangements. Furthermore, international peacekeeping forces would have to be composed of people drawn from many countries and given international citizenship rights and status. This is a different concept from the military forces empowered by United Nations decision to carry out various policing functions, as these have typically been composed of contingents from designated national armed forces.

What economic conversion capability will be needed to assure a disarmament process? In this brief discussion I have emphasized the importance of closing down all military-specific production at the very start of a disarmament process. In order to consider this option on its merits for assuring the reliability of the disarmament process, it will be necessary to have in hand a planning mechanism for converting military industry, bases, laboratories, and other facilities to civilian use. The 1987 law initiated by Rep. Ted Weiss (Dem., NY), H.R. 813, in the US Congress is a useful model for such planning capability. In the absence of prepared plans for moving from military to civilian economy, that fact would be the basis for substantial withholding of political support from a disarmament process. The presence of such conversion plans will play an important political role in each country in assuring support for participation in disarmament. I know of no government that would be prepared to risk the civil disorder that would be the consequence of casting millions of military serving employees onto the streets as jobless.

6
Epilogue:
The Concealed
Cuban Missile Crisis

The meaning of the October 1962 Cuban missile crisis, an event that shaped the course of our century, has been misread and its lessons obscured.

For twenty-five years two aspects of the crisis were given priority attention: first, the Soviets withdrew their missiles from Cuba; second, the style and strategy of the White House deliberations during the fateful week of October 22–28, 1962. The celebration of these accomplishments left a core question virtually unattended: what was the cause of this crisis in the first place? General Maxwell G. Taylor, chairman of the Joint Chiefs of Staff under Kennedy, has asked: "Why, oh, why did he [Khrushchev] put the missiles in in the first place?" If the Soviets had succeeded in emplacing short and intermediate-range weapons in Cuba in 1962, what would they have accomplished?

In his account of President Kennedy's short tenure, Theodore Sorensen, the president's speech writer and confidant, listed fourteen possible reasons that were conjectured in the White House to explain the Soviet move. But that list of speculations meant no explanation.

The attempt to emplace medium and intermediate-range missiles in Cuba made solid sense for the Soviets. For their leaders it was a necessary response to a desperate military situation into which the Soviets had been cornered by a series of remarkable American successes with military materiel and military intelligence.

By the end of 1962 the US had more than 300 land-based intercontinental missiles and a fleet of Polaris missile submarines. The Soviets had four to six land-based ICBMs (1962 White House estimate) and about 100 short-range V-1 type missiles that could be launched from surfaced submarines. Planes: the US had 600 B52s, 600 B47s, 100 B58s (supersonic), all jets with intercontinental range; the USSR had about 200 long-range bombers.

The United States had more than 1700 major nuclear delivery vehicles, to the Soviet's 300. The military realities of 1962 contradicted the "missile gap" falsehood that helped Kennedy win the White House.

Equally important, the US had outmaneuvered and outscored the Soviets in military intelligence. For sixteen months prior to his arrest on the first day of the Cuban missile crisis (October 22, 1962), Colonel Oleg Penkovsky functioned as an American-British intelligence agent. He was a colonel in Soviet Intelligence, deputy head of the Foreign Department of the Committee on Science and Technology of the Council of Ministers, a graduate of the Soviet missile school (ranking first in his class), a member of the elite of Soviet society, having access to the highest levels of officers and security information. The proceedings of his trial in April 1963 revealed that he had delivered 5,000 frames of film of Soviet military-technical information, apart from many hours of talk with western agents during several trips to western Europe. His trial and execution in April 1963 were followed by shakeups in many top military assignments and by a world-wide upheaval in Soviet military intelligence operations.

At some time between August, when he was placed under close surveillance, and October, 1962, the Soviet high command had strong grounds for concluding that knowledge in the hands of Oleg Penkovsky was also in the hands of the US government. Soviet top officers, trained in nuclear military doctrine, had to conclude that the US then possessed decisive advantage in arms and intelligence, and that the USSR no longer wielded a credible nuclear deterrent. That inference was surely reinforced by open discussion among American "defense intellectuals" about the merits of a "first strike" in nuclear war, and by the confident adoption of a flexible nuclear war-fighting strategy by the president and his secretary of defense.

All this meant that the restoration of a credible Soviet nuclear weapons threat was urgently required. This was almost obtained by the Soviet effort to place short and intermediate-range missiles in Cuba.

The Cuban site was especially suited: ninety miles from the US mainland; bypassing the main US ICBM warning system located to the north; within range of southeastern US cities and bases; affording secure control of missiles (even if warheads were stored in Soviet submarines offshore); a coordinated operation for transporting and emplacing the missile batteries could be carried off within two months. All this would have given the Soviet military an impressive number of missiles close enough to the US to be visible and credible, thereby restoring a Soviet nuclear deterrent capability. This was a Soviet alternative to appearing on bended knee before the US.

The Kennedy White House, knowing the overwhelming US arms and military intelligence superiority vis-a-vis the Soviets had even ordered a study on the feasibility of a military first strike on the USSR. The study concluded that this could be done, but there was no way of guaranteeing against the possible destruction of two or more American coastal cities. The idea was dropped as a White House project.

The logic of these data and of contemporary military doctrine is that the Cuban missile crisis grew out of the desperate effort by Soviet leaders to restore nuclear deterrent capability which had been checkmated by US military successes in armaments and intelligence. When large societies with many able people are threatened, then alternative ideas are invented for responding, even to unprecedented problems.

This understanding of the missile crisis does not accord with the characteristic hubris of the Kennedy White House staff and its overconfident judgment—to the point of self-deceit—about the shrewdness and wisdom of the negotiation scenario that finally concluded the missile crisis. The Cuban missile crisis has been used as a model event by American ideologues and arms race planners to teach "crisis management" and to justify escalating military budgets and reliance on arms as a primary instrument of international policy.

Since 1962 various Soviet officials have claimed that Khrushchev's personal "adventurism" was responsible for the Cuban missile crisis. That does not square with what we know of the workings of top Soviet (and US) decision-making. After Stalin, no single person could order such an unprecedented and hazardous move. For Soviet leaders that story has served as a cover for the uncomfortable reality of their 1962 military vulnerability.

For domestic reasons in each case neither Soviet nor American top leaders were prepared to go public with the military facts that lay behind the Cuban Missile Crisis. On the Soviet side there was surely reluctance to reveal that the Soviet ICBM force consisted of only four to six missiles. How would a population react to the disclosure of this meager result after having been marshalled to make heavy economic sacrifices for defense since the close of World War II? On the US side the White House was obviously unwilling to disclose to the American people the military facts of the US-USSR confrontation as that would explode the myth of the "missile gap" that was so serviceable to Kennedy in the 1960 election. Such disclosure would also contradict the political ideology that defined the US government as merely reacting to Soviet military initiatives.

After October 1962 the Soviets proceeded to build up their nuclear delivery forces, as their economy permitted, finally reaching strategic parity with the US. The sobering lesson is that in the nuclear age the old slogans of political domination through military buildups ring hollow, and limits of military power, when disregarded, invite frightful consequences.

Selected Readings

CHAPTER 1.
*Prologue: Economic Consequences of the Arms Race:
The Second Rate Economy.*

Choate, Pat, and Walter, Susan. *America in Ruins.* Washington, DC: The Council of State Planning Agencies, 1981.

DiFilippo, Anthony. *Military Spending and Industrial Decline: A Study of the American Machine Tool Industry.* Westport, Conn.: Greenwood Press, 1986.

Dumas, Lloyd J. *The Over-Burdened Economy.* Los Angeles: University of California Press, 1987, ch. 1. The data appearing on pp. 10 & 11 were subsequently revised and corrected by the author who can be reached at the University of Texas, Dallas, Texas.

Melman, Seymour. *Dynamic Factors in Industrial Productivity.* Oxford and New York: Basil Blackwell, John Wiley, 1956.

———. *Our Depleted Society.* New York: Holt, Rhinehart and Winston, 1965.

———. *Profits Without Production.* New York: Alfred A. Knopf, 1983; Philadelphia: University of Pennsylvania Press, 1987.

———. *The Permanent War Economy.* New York: Simon and Schuster, 1985.

———. *Conversion from Military to Civilian Economy: An Economic Alternative to the Arms Race.* Washington, DC: National SANE Education Fund, 1987.

Physician Task Force on Hunger in America. *Hunger Reaches Blue Collar America.* Cambridge, Mass.: Harvard School of Public Health, 1987.

Ullmann, John E. *The Prospects of American Industrial Recovery.* Westport, Conn.: Quorum Books, 1985.

US Congress, House of Representatives. H.R. 813: "A Bill to Facilitate the Economic Adjustment of Communities, Industries, and Workers to Reductions or Realignments in Defense or Aerospace Contracts, Military Facilities, and Arms Exports, and for Other Purposes." 100th Congress, first session. January 28, 1987.

US Congress, Joint Economic Committee. *The US Trade Position in High Technology: 1980–86.* Washington, DC: Quick, Finan, and Associates, October 1986.

US Department of Commerce, Bureau of Census. *Statistical Abstract of the US for 1985*, 1985.

123

US Department of Defense, Office of the Assistant Secretary of Defense (Comptroller). *National Defense Budget Estimates for FY 1987*. May 1986.

CHAPTER 2.
An Economic Alternative to the Arms Race: Conversion from Military to Civilian Economy

Bluestone, Irving. "Problems of the Worker in Industrial Conversion." In *Journal of Arms Control*, 1:3 (1963), 589–596.

California Public Policy Center. *Jobs from the Sun: Employment Development in the California Solar Energy Industry*. February 1978. 119 pp. From California Public Policy Center, 304 S. Broadway, Room 224, Los Angeles, CA 90013.

Cambern, John R., and Newton, David A. "Skill Transfers: Can Defense Workers Adapt to Civilian Occupations?" In *Monthly Labor Review*. 92 (June 1969), 21–25.

Dumas, Lloyd J. "Economic Conversion, Productive Efficiency and Social Welfare." In *Journal of Sociology and Social Welfare*. 4 (Jan.–Mar. 1977), 567–596.

———, ed. *The Political Economy of Arms Reduction: Reversing Economic Decay*. AAAS Selected Symposium 80, 1982. Westview Press, Inc., 5500 Central Ave., Boulder, CO 80301.

———. *The Overburdened Economy*. Berkeley & Los Angeles: University of California Press, 1986.

Eaton, B. Curtis. "Do Defense Engineers Have Special Reemployment Problems?" In *Monthly Labor Review*. 94 (July 1971), 52–54.

Elliott, D. *The Lucas Aerospace Workers' Campaign*. Young Fabian Pamphlet 46, Nov. 1977. Civic Press Ltd., Civic St., Glasgow G4 9RH, Scotland.

———, Kaldor, M., Smith, D., and Smith, R. *Alternative Work for Military Industries*. Richardson Institute for Conflict and Peace Research, 158 N. Gower St., London NW1 2ND, England, August 1977.

Gordon, S., and McFadden, D., eds. *Economic Conversion: Revitalizing America's Economy*. Cambridge, MA: Ballinger Publishing Co., 1984.

Gutteridge, W. F. "Problems of Conversion of Scientists and Technologists in the Event of Disarmament." Dept. of Languages and Social Science, Lanchester College of Technology, Coventry, England, 1967.

H.R. 813, a bill introduced to the 100th Congress, 1st Session, January 28, 1987, by Congressman Ted Weiss (Dem., NY).

Leitenberg, M. "The Conversion Potential of Military Research and Development Expenditures." In *Bulletin of Peace Proposals*. 51:1 (1974), 73–87.

Melman, Seymour. *Barriers to Conversion from Military to Civilian Industry—in Market, Planned, and Developing Economies*. Prepared for the United Nations Centre for Disarmament, Ad Hoc Group of Governmental Experts on the Relationship between Disarmament and Development, April 1980. (Available from Prof. S. Melman, 304 Mudd, Columbia University, New York, NY 10027.)

———. "Swords into Ploughshares." In *Technology Review*. 89:1 (Jan. 1986), 62–71.

———. "Problems of Conversion from Military to Civilian Economy, An Agenda of Topics, Questions, and Hypotheses." In *Bulletin of Peace Proposals*. 16:1 (1985), 11–19.

———. "Beating Swords into Subways." In *The New York Times Magazine*. Nov. 19, 1978.

———, ed. *Conversion of Industry from a Military to Civilian Economy*, a series in 6 volumes. New York: Frederick Praeger Special Studies, 1970:

> Berkowitz, M. *The Conversion of Military-Oriented R&D to Civilian Uses.*
>
> Christodoulou, A. *Conversion of Nuclear Facilities from Military to Civilian Uses.*
>
> Lynch, J. E. *Local Economic Development after Military Base Closures.*
>
> Mack-Forlist, D. M., and Newman, A. *The Conversion of Shipbuilding from Military to Civilian Markets.*
>
> Melman, S., ed. *The Defense Economy.*
>
> Ullmann, John E., ed. *Potential Civilian Markets for the Military-Electronics Industry.*

———. "Economic Alternatives to Arms Prosperity." In *Annals of the American Academy of Political and Social Sciences*. 351 (Jan. 1964), 121–131.

———. "Inflation and Unemployment as Products of War Economy: The Trade Union Stake in Economic Conversion and Industrial Reconstruction." In *Bulletin of Peace Proposals*. 9:4 (1978), 359–374.

———. *Our Depleted Society*. New York: Holt, Rinehart and Winston and Dell Books, 1965, chs. 10–14.

———. *Planning for Conversion of Military-Industrial and Military Base Facilities*. Washington, DC: Dept. of Commerce, Economic Administration, Office of Technical Assistance, 1973.

———. *The Permanent War Economy*. New York: Simon & Schuster, 1985, chs. 8, 9.

————, ed. *The War Economy of the United States.* New York: St. Martin's Press, 1971, chs. 26–33.

————. *Profits Without Production.* New York: A.A. Knopf, 1983.

Perroux, Francois. "Disarmament and Its Economic Consequences for the Atomic and Aerospace Industries." In Emile Benoit and Nils Peter Gleditsch, eds., *Disarmament and World Economic Interdependence.* New York: Columbia University Press, 1967, 154–160.

Reich, Michael, and Finkelhor, David. "Capitalism and the Military Industrial Complex: The Obstacles to Conversion." In Richard Edwards, Michael Reich, and Thomas Weisskopf, eds., *The Capitalist System: A Radical Analysis of American Society.* Englewood Cliffs, N.J.: Prentice Hall, 1972.

Sense About Defence: The Report of the Labour Party Defence Study Group. Quartet Books Ltd., 27 Goodge St., London W1P 1FD, England, 1977. [Note: includes a major listing of studies on the UK military economy and economic conversion prospects and problems.—S.M.]

Shearer, D. "Swords into Plowshares: A Program for Conversion." In *Working Papers for a New Society.* 2 (Summer 1973), 51–61.

Thorsson, Inga. *In Pursuit of Disarmament: Conversion from Military to Civil Production in Sweden.* Stockholm: Liber Allmanna Forlaget, vols. 1a and 1b, 1984, vol. 2, 1985.

US Arms Control and Disarmament Agency. *Community Readjustment to Reduced Defense Spending: Case Studies of Potential Impact on Seattle-Tacoma, Baltimore, and New London-Groton-Norwich.* Washington, DC: GPO, May 1966.

US Comptroller General. *Problems Associated with Converting Defense Research Facilities to Meet Different Needs. The Case of Fort Detrick.* Report to the Congress, B-160140, Feb. 16, 1972.

US Dept. of Defense, Office of Economic Adjustment. *Economic Recovery: Community Response to Defense Decisions to Close Bases.* 1976.

Wallensteen, P., ed. *Experiences in Disarmament: On Conversion of Military Industry and Closing of Military Bases.* Report No. 19, June 1978. Dept. of Peace and Conflict Research, Uppsala University, Uppsala, Sweden. [Note: contains major review article on conversion literature, papers on US, UK, and Sweden, and bibliographic appendices.—S.M.]

Wong, C. *Economic Consequences of Armament and Disarmament—A Bibliography.* Center for the Study of Armament and Disarmament, California State University, Los Angeles, CA 90032, 1981.

CHAPTER 3.
Politics for Peace:
A Road Map, Not a STOP Sign

Boyer, P. *By the Bomb's Early Light: American Thought and Culture at the Dawn of the Atomic Age.* New York: Pantheon Books, 1985.

Feshbach, S. and White, M.J. "Individual Differences in Attitudes Towards Nuclear Arms Policies: Some Psychological and Social Policy Considerations." In *Journal of Peace Research*, vol. 23, no. 2 (June, 1986).

Sandman, P.M. and Valenti, J.M. "Scared Stiff or Scared into Action." In *Bulletin of the Atomic Scientists* (January 1986).

War-Making Institutions

Barnet, R. *The Roots of War.* Markham, Ont.: Penguin Books, 1972, chs. 2–4, 7.

Chomsky, N. *Towards A New Cold War.* New York: Pantheon Books, 1982.

———. *Turning the Tide: US Intervention in Central America and the Struggle for Peace.* Boston: South End Press, 1986.

———. *The Chomsky Reader.* New York: Pantheon Books, 1987.

Dibble, V.K. "The Garrison Society." In *New University Thought,* nos. 66–67, 1967.

Gansler, J. *The Defense Industry.* Cambridge: MIT Press, 1980, ch. 2.

Melman, S. *Pentagon Capitalism.* New York: McGraw-Hill, 1970, chs. 1–4.

———. *The Permanent War Economy.* New York: Simon & Schuster, 1985, chs. 3, 10.

Oakes, W.J. "Toward A Permanent War Economy." In *The War Economy of the US,* edited by S. Melman. New York: St.Martin's Press, 1971.

Raskin, M. "Democracy Versus the National Security State." In *Law and Contemporary Problems,* 1976.

Wise, D. and Ross, T.B. In *The Invisible Government.* New York: Random House, 1964.

War Economy and Consequences

DeGrasse, R. *Military Expansion, Economic Decline.* Council on Economic Priorities, New York 1983.

Dumas, L.J. *The Overburdened Economy.* Los Angeles: University of California Press, 1986.

Melman, S. *The Permanent War Economy.* New York: Simon & Schuster, 1985.

———. *Profits Without Production.* New York: Alfred A. Knopf, 1983.
Ullmann, J.E. *The Prospects of American Industrial Recovery.* Westport, Conn.: Quorum Books, 1985.

Economic Conversion

Gordon, S., and McFadden, D., eds. *Economic Conversion: Revitalizing America's Economy.* Cambridge: Ballinger Publishing Co., 1984.
H.R. 229, a bill introduced to the 99th Congress, 1st Session, January 3, 1985, by Congressman Ted Weiss (Dem., NY).
Melman, S. *Barriers to Conversion from Military to Civilian Industry—in Market, Planned, and Developing Economies.* (Prepared for the United Nations Centre for Disarmament, April 1980, and available from Prof. S. Melman, 304 Mudd, Columbia University, New York, NY 10027.)
———. "Swords into Ploughshares." In *Technology Review*, 89:1 (Jan. 1986).
———. "Problems of Conversion from Military to Civilian Economy, An Agenda of Topics, Questions, and Hypotheses." In *Bulletin of Peace Proposals*, 16:1 (1985).

Disarmament

Melman, S. *Disarmament, Its Politics and Economics.* American Academy of Arts and Sciences, 1962.
Myrdal, A. *The Game of Disarmament.* New York: Pantheon Books, 1976.
Raskin, M. *Draft Treaty for a Comprehensive Program for Common Security and General Disarmament*, 1986. (Available from Marcus Raskin, Institute for Policy Studies, 1901 Q St., NW, Washington, DC 20009.)

Worker Ownership

Frieden, K. *Workplace Democracy and Productivity.* National Center for Economic Alternatives, 1980.
Jackall, R. and Levin, H.M., eds. *Worker Cooperatives in America.* Los Angeles: University of California Press, 1984.
Thomas, H. and Logan, C. *Mondragon, an Economic Analysis.* London: George Allen & Unwin, 1982.
Zwerdling, D. *Workplace Democracy.* Harper, 1978.

CHAPTER 4.   (No readings for Chapter 4.)

CHAPTER 5.
Strategic Factors for Designing a Disarmament Process

US and USSR 1962 plans. Full texts, in *Disarmament: Its Politics and Economics*, edited by S. Melman, pp. 279–331.

Aronowitz, D. *Legal Aspects of Arms Control Verification in the US.* New York: Oceana, 1985

Barnet, R. *Who Wants Disarmament?* Kansas City: Beacon, 1960.

Berman, H.J. and Maggs, P.B. *Disarmament Inspection Under Soviet Law.* New York: Oceana, 1967.

Burns, R.D. *Arms Control and Disarmament: a Bibliography.* New York: CLIO Press, 1977.

Clark, G., and Sohn, L.B. *World Peace Through World Law*, 2nd edition (revised). Boston: Harvard University Press, 1964.

Falk, R., and Barnet, R., eds. *Security in Disarmament.* Princeton: Princeton University Press, 1965.

Henkin, L. *Arms Control and Inspection in American Law*, New York: Columbia, 1958.

McKnight, A. and Suter, K. *The Forgotten Treaties.* The Law Council of Australia, 1983.

McVitty, M.H. *Preface to Disarmament: An Appraisal of Recent Proposals.* Washington: Public Affairs Press, 1970.

Melman, S., ed. *Disarmament: Its Politics and Economics.* The American Academy of Arts and Sciences, 1962.

———, ed. *Inspection for Disarmament.* New York: Columbia University Press, 1958.

Myrdal, A. *The Game of Disarmament.* New York: Pantheon, 1976.

Noel-Baker, P. *The Arms Race.* South Lancaster, MA.: Atlantic Books, 1958.

Raskin, M. *The Common Good.* New York: Routledge, Chapman Hall, 1986.

———. *Draft Treaty for a Comprehensive Program for Common Security and General Disarmament.* Institute for Policy Studies, 1986.

Spanier, J.W., and Noge, J.L. *The Politics of Disarmament.* New York: Praeger, 1962.

United Nations. *Disarmament Yearbook*, a series.

US Arms Control and Disarmament Agency, annual reports.

Index

131

The Author

Seymour Melman has a worldwide reputation in the fields of industrial productivity, conversion from military to civilian industry, and the social costs of militarism. Early studies on the economic factors that determine the design and use of technology, and resulting productivity, are reflected in his books, *Dynamic Factors in Industrial Productivity* (1956) and *Decision-Making and Productivity* (1958). Professional experience, combined with a commitment to peaceful solutions to human problems drew him unavoidably to the challenge of reversing the arms race. This phase is mirrored in the published works, *Inspection For Disarmament* (1958) and *The Peace Race* (1961). Subsequent studies of weaponry, economic consequences of military policies, and workable paths to conversion from military to civilian economy ripened into such volumes as *Our Depleted Society* (1965), *Pentagon Capitalism* (1970) and *The Permanent War Economy* (1974, 1985). His most recent book, *Profits Without Production* (1983, 1988) is an analysis of the characteristics of private and government managers of military and civilian industries and the effect of their policies on industrial and wider societal competence.

Professor Melman has been associated with Columbia University for four decades, receiving his first instructorship there in the Department of Industrial Engineering and Operations Research in 1948, his doctorate in economics in 1949, his professorship in 1963. Professor Emeritus since 1988, he continues to preside over seminars and remains active in his fields of interest, notably as chairman of the National Commission for Economic Conversion and Disarmament, Washington, D.C. He is the recipient of many awards, including Honorary member of the Faculty, Industrial College of the Armed Forces, and he only recently concluded fifteen years as co-chair of SANE, America's largest peace organization.